FIN

ALASKA'S

VILLAGES

AND CONNECTING THEM

ALEX HILLS

First published by Dog Ear Publishing
4011 Vincennes Rd
Indianapolis, IN 46268
www.dogearpublishing.net

ISBN: 978-1-4575-5110-9

This book is printed on acid-free paper.

Printed in the United States of America

Same as *Wi-Fi and the Bad Boys of Radio*, including:

This book is a work of nonfiction based on actual events. The author and publisher make no explicit guarantee as to the accuracy of the information contained in the book, although every effort has been made to be as historically authentic and error-free as possible. Some passages are similar to or the same as passages in *Wi-Fi and the Bad Boys of Radio: Dawn of a Wireless Technology*, whose copyright is held by the author of this book.

Dedication

For the young pioneers
who will follow the path of these Alaskan heroes
but don't yet imagine all that they can achieve.

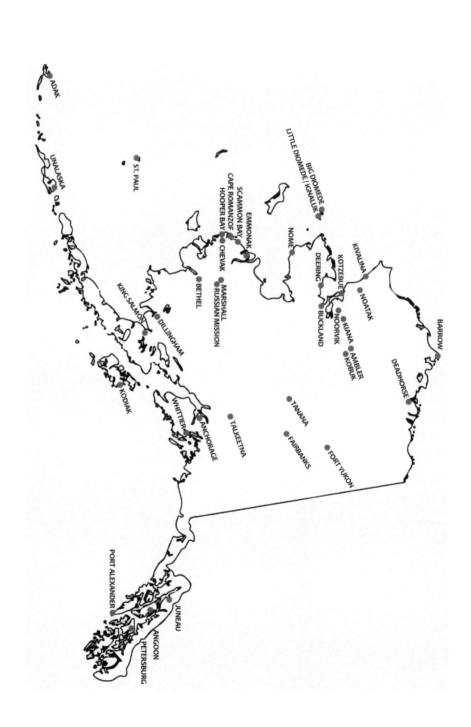

TABLE OF CONTENTS

FOREWORD

Alaska's telecommunication systems have been built — or attempted to be built — by colorful characters, smart people and innovators who've changed the world. Success has also depended on working well with families who have lived in Alaska for 10,000 years — Alaska Natives — who have welcomed new connections across this vast, cold place, but who, often in the same breath, want to be sure that their own languages and customs are preserved and protected.

Throughout this history, there have been some common themes:

- First, Alaska is a proving ground.

- A second theme in Alaska telecom history has been intense competition.

- A third common theme in this history of Alaska telecommunications is that we've tended to attract some colorful, hardy, visionary and inventive characters.

- The fourth theme in Alaska's telecom history is that Alaskans themselves have consistently welcomed improvements.

This new book by Alex Hills amplifies all of these themes. After serving in Korea as a U.S. military officer, Alex arrived in Alaska and soon found himself in the state's "phone wars." But he was consistently on the side of advancing technology — sometimes finding ways to make old technology work and sometimes helping to create new technology. He encountered life-threatening challenges and ornery bureaucrats with the sense of humor displayed in these pages. He has, again and again, been in uncomfortable situations and come out with innovation.

Alex came to Alaska with the perspective that anything is possible if you keep working the problem. He puts no limits on his thinking, and he uses his imagination. He's as comfortable in a Silicon Valley boardroom as climbing a tower in Bethel or leading his students to a remote part of the world — Malawi in southern Africa or an Amazon jungle town in Peru, for example.

When I first met Alex, I wasn't surprised to find that an Alaskan had led the team that built the first large Wi-Fi network. Since then I've worked with Alex in several settings: as a member of the Alaska Science and Technology Foundation Board in the late 1990s, developing a wireless location-based technology at Venture Ad Astra, establishing the Alaska Innovator's Hall of Fame, and now serving with him on Iridium's Polar Advisory Board, where we're helping to build a global satellite network to help solve communication problems in the north.

Reading this book told me more about Alex than I'd learned over coffee in the last 20 years, and helps me understand the human element behind our phone systems, more than any other account of telecommunications in Alaska. Now I'll be sure I don't take for granted that phone call to rural Alaska — ever!

Mead Treadwell
President, Pt Capital
Lt. Governor of Alaska, 2010-2014
Commissioner, U.S. Arctic Research Commission, 2001-2010
Chair, U.S. Arctic Research Commission, 2006-2010
Anchorage, Alaska
September 2016

Note: A supplement to this Foreword appears near the end of the book. See Table of Contents.

PREFACE

I was a lucky guy. When I first set foot in Alaska, big things were about to happen. I had arrived just in time for the decade of the 1970s.

In 1971 the Alaska Native Claims Settlement Act was signed into law, settling aboriginal land claims, clearing the way for construction of the trans-Alaska oil pipeline, and triggering a big upswing in the young state's economy. By 1977, when the first oil flowed through the pipeline, Alaska was already starting to change.

Another landmark happened in 1971. The RCA Corporation purchased Alaska's long-distance telephone system. Then called the Alaska Communications System — the ACS — it was operated by the U.S. Air Force. As part of the ACS purchase, RCA agreed to provide phone service to Alaska's villages, a service that hadn't previously been available to most of them. The ACS purchase, combined with some serendipitous circumstances, set in motion a series of events that led to the delivery of modern telecommunication services to the villages.

And by 1971 Alaska had already recognized the benefits of public broadcasting — then called "educational broadcasting" — and created the Alaska Educational Broadcasting Commission. The new agency was poised to foster a new network of broadcast stations to serve the many Alaska communities then with no existing radio or television service, setting the stage for another new service for the villages.

By the end of the decade, Alaska's rural villages were well on their way to receiving broadcast radio and television, telephone service for all, and reliable medical communication links. But the path to full modern telecommunication service was not a smooth one. The journey along that rocky road is the story that waits in the pages ahead.

This is not a complete Alaska telecommunication history — or even a complete telecommunication history of the 1970s. It's just a personal story based on my experiences from 1972 to 1976. It's a remembrance of the great people I knew and worked with during that period, people who became my friends. And it's a story of how I found rural Alaska and its villages — and how I discovered its people — some of the finest I've ever known.

You're about to read the experiences of a young engineer who sought adventure in Alaska — and found it!

ACKNOWLEDGMENTS

There were many who worked on developing Alaska's telecommunication systems in the 1970s, but only some of them appear in this book. The absence of others certainly does not diminish the importance of their work. It only reflects the book's focus on my personal experiences and the stories of those with whom I worked directly.

I am indebted to those who patiently answered my questions, reviewed drafts, provided advice, checked facts, and gave encouragement. They are: Brian Beard, David Cheezem, Richard Chiappone, Cathy Hiebert, Karen Hills, Rebecca Hills, John Lee, Greg Moore, Nellie (Ward) Moore, Doug Neal, Cecil Sanders, and Lee Wareham.

I am also indebted to Heather E. Hudson, whose book, *Connecting Alaskans: Telecommunications in Alaska from Telegraph to Broadband*, helped with some of the fine points of Alaska's telecommunication history, and to Robin Chlupach, for her book, *Airwaves Over Alaska: The Story of Broadcaster Augie Hiebert*, which details my friend Augie Hiebert's many contributions.

But my greatest debt is to the beautiful young nurse I found in Alaska. My wife Meg has long put up with my strange ways, including those she's tolerated during the writing of this book. I'm deeply grateful.

Alex Hills
Palmer Alaska
September 2016

1

ANCHORAGE

SEPTEMBER 1972

Tiny waves lapped against the red and white seaplane's silver-colored floats. The plane bobbed in the water.

I pulled on my rubber hip boots — extra long to accommodate my extra long legs — untied the plane from the dock, and climbed up into my seat. The pilot sat to my left.

"Ready?" he asked.

"All set."

"Clear!" he shouted.

The engine started, and the Cessna began to move slowly.

Pilot John Lee spoke into the radio's microphone. "Anchorage tower, Cessna seven-zero-zero-two-two taxiing for departure Lake Hood."

The tower radioed takeoff clearance. John pushed the throttle forward, the engine roared, and we rushed down the watery runway. The Cessna broke free of the water and banked right. We headed toward western Alaska.

1-1 A Cessna 185 ready to taxi and take off at Lake Hood.

We were outbound from Lake Hood, Anchorage's airport for float-equipped planes capable of landing on the myriad bodies of water strewn across Alaska. The watery air strip is a canal cut between two lakes beside Anchorage International Airport, host to big commercial jets bound for smaller states, Europe, and Asia.

On instructions from the tall tower at Anchorage International, a little float plane can taxi from its dock, line up on the canal runway, and fly off to remote parts of Alaska, later landing on a convenient bay, lake, or river.

I had come north in search of adventure after first using my engineering degree to get a job as a member of the design team building what was then the world's fastest computer. But I wanted more excitement. After a few years of military service in Korea, and another few years in graduate school and traveling around the U.S. as an itinerant engineering instructor, I still wasn't satisfied. I headed north to Alaska and finally found the adventure I was seeking — leading the team installing the first telephones in Alaska's remote villages.

Looking down, I saw a few small villages dotting the tundra below. Nestled along coasts and rivers, Alaska's hundreds of villages were home to Alaska Natives, comprising three major groups — Eskimos in Alaska's north and west,[1] Indians in the interior, southcentral and southeast parts of Alaska,[2] and Aleuts in the southwest islands that are strung out like a necklace along the archipelago called the Aleutian Islands.

In 1972 few of the villages had a reliable communication system, and none had telephones. There were some shortwave radios, but shortwave signals are disrupted by the *aurora borealis* — the "northern lights" so common in the far north. The wispy green and red curtains fluttering across the northern sky put on a fascinating show, but their beauty was no comfort to shortwave radio users frustrated by communication interruptions that could last for days or weeks.

I led the field installation crew of the "bush telephone program." Our job was to put a single VHF radio telephone in each village. With the help of antennas that looked like 1950s rooftop TV contraptions turned on their sides, the radio phone equipment sent signals to radio base stations, relaying callers' voices to Alaska's telephone network. The VHF system was more reliable than a shortwave.

We were a small band of techies. With an airplane, tools and equipment, we flew from Alaska's south to north and back again, installing a single radio phone in each village. Each phone had to be shared by an entire village, and, in most cases, it was a village's first experience with modern telephone service.

The phone could be used to call a nearby town to order supplies or spare parts. It could be used to call Junior, attending school

1-2 The *aurora borealis* puts on a light show in the northern sky.

hundreds or even thousands of miles away at a Bureau of Indian Affairs boarding school. And, when an urgent medical situation arose, the phone could be used to reliably call a doctor or request an airplane for medical evacuation. It was a welcome addition.[3]

John and I had bonded as we flew to and from the villages. We had both been Army Signal Corps officers and company commanders. He served in Vietnam. I served in South Korea. And we both knew radio technology. Installer-technicians moved in and out of our team, but we remained on the job. We were friends.

This was a site survey trip. Before I could bring in other team members to install equipment, I needed to choose the best place in each village for the equipment and antenna. Officially the team's pilot, John was also an engineer. He helped me design antenna installations. And he helped me find the best location in each village to install the antenna and equipment. Our plan for this trip was to survey more than 20 villages.

We landed on the Yukon River at Emmonak, a village of about 450 people with houses sprawled across the flats near the mouth of the great river. After we tied up the Cessna, John set out in search of good locations for our installation. My task was to find the village chief, mayor, or someone else in charge. In Emmonak I was looking for Axel Johnson, the village council president.[4]

As we set off in separate directions, John smirked, "You really like that PR work, don't you?"

He liked to kid me about doing "public relations" work. But my work with local officials was important. I explained the bush telephone program to each local leader, and we later reached agreement on where our equipment would be located and connected to electrical power. I asked each local leader to choose from among the sites that John suggested.

But it seemed that the company's lawyers had been working overtime. I was required to ask each village official to sign an agreement saying that the village would provide space and electrical power at no charge. The lawyers thought that, after the novelty of the new telephone was gone, villages would ask to be compensated for the space and power they were providing. The lawyers were worried about the company's liability. But I wasn't concerned. The villagers were gracious people. They just wanted to be helpful.

The radio phone equipment had originally been designed for the trunk of a car. Before cell phones, a customer could have a mobile phone installed in a car. The telephone handset and control unit were placed under the car's dashboard, and the bulky radio equipment was in the trunk.

It was a service never widely used by the public, but the equipment was what we needed. We adapted it to be installed in a village building and connected it to an old-fashioned black wall phone with a rotary dial. Like the Ma Bell of long ago,[5] we allowed villagers to choose a wall phone of any color — as long as it was black.

John looked for a central place in each village for the telephone. A convenient place like the general store or medical clinic was ideal if it had a clear radio shot to the nearest radio base station.[6]

After finishing our work in Emmonak, we headed to Bethel, a bigger town of about 2500 people that was our base when we worked in the villages of southwest Alaska. John and I both looked forward to a cold beer and a good night's sleep.

In Bethel, with the sun dropping toward the northwest horizon, John refueled the Cessna at a dock on the bank of the Kuskokwim River. I watched from a nearby seawall made of big rocks heaped along the riverbank to slow the river's nibbling the bank. But there was a mix-up between John and the fuel attendant. The attendant untied the plane from the dock before John was ready to restart the engine. Suddenly the Cessna was drifting downstream toward a big barge. And the engine wasn't running!

Standing on a float as the plane drifted downstream, John looked surprised. He and the Cessna needed help. It was time to do something!

John scrambled. He threw me a line. To grab it, I dropped down lower on the seawall with the top of my hip boots dipping below the waterline. John looped the line around a cleat on the Cessna's float. And I pulled — hard.

As I hauled the plane back toward the dock, water rushed into my boots. The cold water chilled my legs and feet, but John had the look of a grateful pilot. At the small cost of wet feet, we had saved the Cessna from serious damage that would have caused work delays. It would also have been hard to explain to our bosses in Anchorage.

An hour later we drank beer and congratulated ourselves on some quick action that avoided a small disaster. But it wouldn't be our last close call.

1-3 John and I had a little mishap as the sun set over Bethel.

The next day we flew off to survey Marshall, Russian Mission, and other villages along the lower Yukon River.

John asked, "You really like these Native folks, don't you?"

"Yeah, I guess I do."

"I thought so."

"A couple years ago," I continued, "I turned down a chance to join the Peace Corps to bring electric power systems to Central America. But this is better. I like the people here."

My work on the bush telephone project had started a few months earlier. It was a commercial venture, but there was also a higher purpose.

The job wasn't just about a paycheck. It was a mission.

2

SCAMMON BAY

JULY 1972

Two months earlier we were having signal reception problems in the villages of Scammon Bay, Hooper Bay, and Chevak, all huddled near the coast of the Bering Sea. The worst of the problems was at Scammon Bay, which lay beside its namesake bay that opened into the Bering. I was spending lots of time in that little village.

We circled and then lined up to make a landing. I could see people standing beside the airstrip.

I stepped from the plane and heard young voices ask, "What can we carry?"

It happened every time we arrived in Scammon Bay. The teenagers wanted to help by carrying my toolboxes into the village. The kids spoke the English they learned and used in school, but most of the village elders spoke only the Cup'ik dialect of their native language Yup'ik.

As we carried my toolboxes up to the little general store where the radio phone was installed, I saw an elder — a lady — kneeling on the ground and cutting fish. I nodded a hello. Her weathered face was

2-1 We looked down on tundra lakes as we flew toward Scammon Bay.

a deadpan. She was cutting some salmon that had been caught by the men of the village in their subsistence nets, preparing the fish to be dried on outdoor racks. It would be later stored as food for the winter.

One of my teenage escorts whispered, "That's Maryann Sundown!"

Maryann looked down to focus on the salmon in her hands. She deftly cut it with an *ulu*, a traditional knife with a curved cutting edge.[1] When she looked up at me again, her face was still deadpan.

We began to communicate — in a way. Maryann spoke only Cup'ik, and one of the teenagers offered to act as an English-to-Cup'ik interpreter. But Maryann communicated mostly with a wink or a raised eyebrow. As she spoke to me, her voice was expressionless, but her eyes laughed. A few moments passed. Then she flashed a devilish grin.

Later I learned that Maryann was a renowned Native dancer. Her fame had spread across Alaska because her dance performances invariably kept her audiences in stitches. She and her cousin Agnes did the "mosquito dance," in which the two women portrayed berry pickers bedeviled by the pesky bugs. They jumped around and swatted wildly, delighting the audience. Maryann was known as the "Yup'ik Dance Diva of Scammon Bay."

2-2 Maryann Sundown looked up from her work cutting salmon.

Like other elders in the village, Maryann had seen dramatic changes — the arrival of snowmobiles and radios, and later telephones and television. But she was steadfast in holding onto traditional values — belief in family, community and the importance of helping others. Meeting people like her was a bonus I hadn't expected when I signed on to lead the bush telephone program.

Others in the villages received me with warm hospitality. It was typical.

Up and down the Yukon and Kuskokwim rivers, I was asked, "Would you like some *agutaq*?" It's the Yup'ik word for "Eskimo ice cream" — blueberries in whipped reindeer tallow, seal oil and water.[2]

In the north, I was sometimes asked, "How about some *muktuk*?" That's the Inupiaq word for frozen whale skin and blubber.

Once I was offered some walrus flipper. I gratefully accepted it. It was chewy.

To return the hospitality, I bought fresh fruit and vegetables available in the big city of Anchorage, flying them in as gifts to the villages, where they were scarce commodities.

At first I suspected we were so warmly received because people really wanted the new phone service. But later I realized the villagers didn't think that way. Offering such hospitality was standard for them.

A year and a half earlier, a historic event had made our little project possible. That was when the Radio Corporation of America — RCA — had agreed to buy Alaska's long-distance telephone system. It was called the Alaska Communications System — ACS — and it was operated by the U.S. Air Force. The $28.4 million purchase happened on January 10, 1971.

But, as part of the deal, Alaska's state government officials demanded that RCA provide telephone service to small villages spread all across the state. RCA agreed that, within three years of the purchase, the company would provide telephone service to 142 Alaska villages that then had no phone service.[3] [4] RCA set up a subsidiary called RCA Alaska Communications — RCA Alascom — to operate and upgrade the ACS network and to provide telephone service to the villages.[5]

In 1971 rural communication relied on the few shortwave sets that could be found in each village. One of these was used by the village health aide to stay in contact with doctors at a hospital in a regional center somewhere near the village. A second was typically used by the village agent for Wien Air Alaska, which in those days carried the mail and provided scheduled air service — known as the "mail plane" — to the villages. The shortwave radios could also be used to reach one of the RCA's "land radio" stations, which offered telegram service or a "patch" into the telephone network. But shortwave communication was unreliable. RCA's plan was to improve on the shortwave system by putting a VHF radio phone in each village.

A month after I finished working in Scammon Bay, I caught an Alaska Airlines jet and flew to Petersburg, a small fishing town in southeast Alaska that was settled by Norwegian fisherman in the late 19th century. The town revels in its Norwegian traditions. It calls itself "Little Norway."

John was still in Anchorage, preparing the Cessna to follow me to Petersburg. My Alaska Airlines flights had me in Petersburg within six hours, but, for John and the Cessna, the trip would take a full day — and then some.

Petersburg was a regional center — with phones and other modern facilities — that we were to use as our base to install radio phone equipment in three nearby villages. Like Alaska villages in the north, villages in southeast Alaska wanted telephones to

2-3 Each village radio phone used an antenna like this one.

order supplies, groceries and repair parts. People in Alaska's cities —Anchorage, Fairbanks and Juneau — could pick up the phone to place a J.C. Penney order, but folks in the villages had to send their orders by mail.

Transportation in southeast Alaska is not by road. It's by water and air. There are many islands but few bridges connecting them. The Cessna, still on floats, would be our transportation.

John was a few days behind me, and, while I waited for him, I worked at the RCA station in Petersburg, organizing our tools and equipment. The RCA station would be our base for the next few weeks. Soon I had everything in order. I was ready to go. Only John and the technician who was to follow him aboard an Alaska Airlines jet were missing.

Two days passed. I wondered when John and the Cessna would leave Anchorage. Early on the third day a telegram arrived. It said that John was en route to Petersburg. But there was no further communication from him.

I watched the RCA station clock tick off the hours. The afternoon wore on, and the sun fell toward the horizon. I wondered if John had encountered bad weather or other problems.

The sun dove below the horizon. It was abrupt. In northern Alaska a sunset is a gradual affair, with the sky dimming slowly, but Petersburg isn't in the north and this was different. Suddenly it was dark, and there was still no word of John.

Then the RCA station chief handed me a scribbled phone message. John would arrive in an hour. He would land in the Petersburg harbor and tie up at the dock reserved for visiting float planes. That's when I really got worried.

I rooted through our equipment, found two flashlights and galloped to the water's edge. Standing at the end of the dock, I used a light to scan the water.

Between the open area of the harbor, where the Cessna would land, and the float plane dock, there were some big "dolphins" — clusters of pilings sticking out of the water that could be used to tie up boats. Cloud cover obscured the moon, and the dolphins were nearly invisible on that dark night. If John hit one of those dolphins, the Cessna would be damaged, and our project would be delayed. Even if he just dinged a wing, it would put us out of action for a while. And our bosses in Anchorage would not be happy. Just like our close call with that big barge in Bethel.

Soon I saw the Cessna's landing light. The plane was taxiing across the harbor. I imagined John squinting in the darkness, trying to find the floatplane dock. Then he turned toward me! He had seen my light!

The flashlight was a beacon guiding John toward the dock. But it also let him see the hulking dolphins. An interruption in the flashlight's beam told John there was a dolphin between him and me, and he steered around it.

Agonizing minutes passed. As John approached me, he cut the engine, and the Cessna coasted to the dock. The flashlight's beam had been his guide. The Cessna was unscathed.

The next few days were less exciting. Our technician arrived from Anchorage, and the three of us focused on installing radio phone equipment in Port Alexander, Point Baker, and Cape Pole. John and I made plans to fly together to the three villages to do site surveys while the technician stayed in Petersburg to prepare the radio phone equipment for installation.

On the first day we surveyed two villages, Point Baker and Cape Pole, but low clouds prevented our landing at the third one. The next day the weather lifted a bit, and we slipped into Port Alexander, a small fishing village near the south tip of Baranof Island, a big island along southeast Alaska's outer coast. Once a salmon fishing hub and bustling city of 2500, Port Alexander had shrunk to only about 35 people. We touched down just offshore of the village. We tied up the plane and headed off in search of the village's leader.

There was no mayor or city council there, but John Pierce was the recognized leader. He told me that they wanted the phone and its equipment installed in Dick Gore's general store, where the phone would be available to all village residents. The radio coverage at the store looked okay, so John and I went over there to talk with Dick.

He said, "Sure, you can put it here. It's not a problem."

But, by the time our site survey was finished, clouds had descended on Port Alexander, and we could see that there would be no return to Petersburg that day. It wasn't unusual for us to be weathered in at a village. It slowed our work routine, but it was part of the job. We checked the plane to be sure it was tied down securely and then walked back to the general store.

We were invited to dinner by Dick Gore and his wife. They also invited us to spend the night at their house. At dinner I noticed some gouges and scratches on the kitchen wall. I was puzzled until Dick explained that they had an unusual house pet.

He said "It's a margay."

"Really?" I asked. "A wild cat?"

"Yep. A margay is something like an ocelot. It's native to Central and South America."

John's eyebrows jumped up. I wondered where we'd be sleeping that night.

The margay had yellowish-brown fur dotted with black ringed spots. With black ears, it stood about two feet high. And it was not friendly. Dick didn't explain why they had a margay as a pet. We had no interest in stroking the animal's fur.

The Gores' general store was on the first floor of the building, and their living quarters were upstairs on the second and third floors. The main living area and the Gores' bedroom were on the second floor. John and I were to sleep in a third floor attic bedroom.

As we lay there that night, we heard cat feet padding about in the darkness. We couldn't see the animal. We could only hear it. But we imagined it was ready to pounce at any moment. Neither of us slept much.

The next day the weather lifted, and we flew back to Petersburg with no desire to overnight again in Port Alexander.

3

BETHEL

NOVEMBER 1972

The chill in the November air deepened, signaling the approach of winter. It was time to change the Cessna's landing gear.

In September John had removed the plane's floats and replaced them with wheels. But it was time to add skis to the already installed wheels, making a wheel-ski combination that allowed us to land on an airstrip using the wheels or on packed snow using the skis. We flew to Anchorage. I worked in RCA's office for a day while John installed the skis at a nearby airport.

The wheel-ski combination would let us land almost anywhere that was flat and continue to work through the winter months. But winter work in Alaska posed other problems— weather problems, equipment problems, and people problems.

Even when protected by warm winter clothing, people working in frigid conditions move slowly. They need to rest and warm up frequently. Workers who are cold may fail to think clearly, increasing the risk of accidents. I never asked my crew to work outside when the chill temperature dropped below -50 degrees Fahrenheit. The crew didn't think I was being overly kind, but it was a trade-off between efficiency and safety. It was getting the work done while avoiding accidents.

The cold affected mechanical equipment. Motor oil in engines could become as thick as axle grease. We put a small catalytic heater in the engine compartment of the Cessna to keep its engine warm overnight. Or in the morning we warmed the engine with a kerosene heater.

At temperatures below zero degrees Fahrenheit, batteries functioned reluctantly. So we removed the battery from the Cessna each night and kept it in our warm sleeping quarters, installing it again in the morning just before we were ready to take off. And we always stored electronic equipment in heated buildings so it was not exposed to low temperatures.

Bad flying weather — ice, snow, and poor visibility — cost us work time. Even after we cleared the plane's wings of ice and snow, there were winter days when low visibility prevented flying to a village. Winter delays were just part of the bush telephone project.

Rather than return to our base each night and run the risk that the next day's weather would keep us from our village worksite, I decided to keep the crew in each village for the two or three days needed to complete a radio phone installation. I enjoyed those overnight stays, but the technicians were less enthusiastic.

With no inns or hotels in the villages, we often spent nights in sleeping bags in the guest room of a local school or on wrestling mats on the school's gym floor. Sometimes we stayed with families in their homes. Staying overnight in the villages helped us to keep to our schedule, but the company paid a price.

The technicians' union pushed through a labor contract amendment requiring that wages be paid for the entire time they were in a village, including "sleeping bag" time. It was an obvious response to my decision, but I saw it as just the cost of doing business in rural Alaska. RCA's management did not object.

But even with the extra pay, the technicians made it clear they didn't like sleeping in the villages. They just didn't share my enthusiasm for rural Alaska life. I decided to rotate crews. Every few weeks I sent two men back to Anchorage to work in the office and brought out two different technicians to continue the installation work. With the new scheme, the technicians were happier, I was happier, and we stayed on schedule.

Sometimes I visited villages where we had previously installed phones. On one November trip I was surprised to find that an old problem persisted.

Four months earlier, in July, I had reported to RCA headquarters a problem I said threatened the success of the village telephone program. Headquarters promised to follow up. I stopped thinking about the problem and went back to focusing on installing the system and making it work. But in November I found that, in spite of my report, nothing had been done to resolve the problem. That surprised me. I decided to solve things myself.

There was only one phone in each village. All calls placed from a village went to other villages, towns and cities. They were all long-distance calls, and they came with charges. In July I had found that some village telephones were being disconnected because of villages' failure to pay these charges.

At the end of each month, a bill arrived, and the villagers had no money to pay the bill. They didn't understand that there would be long-distance charges. My predecessors on the bush telephone project had never explained this to the villagers! John might have called this "public relations," but it seemed obvious that, with one telephone shared by everyone in a village, a method of accounting was needed to charge long-distance calls to the people who made them. Why hadn't the company antici-pated this need?

When in November I found that the problem was still unre-solved, I created a procedure for handling long-distance charges. I made a telephone log form and an instruction sheet for the vil-lages to use, and I contacted RCA's public relations department, asking them to publish the instruction sheet. The public relations staff distributed the sheet to all of the villages with telephones.

In each village I asked the leader to select a telephone atten-dant to coordinate the use of the telephone, and I taught the attendant how to account for the long-distance calls. At the end of each call, the attendant was to ask the long-distance operator for "time and charges" — the length and cost of the call. The attendant entered this information into the log beside the name of the person who had placed the call. The caller could either pay right away or settle up at the end of the month. With the new system in place, the villages started to pay their bills on time.

RCA, the local telephone companies that did the billing, and the villagers each had a job to do. I showed the villagers how to do their part, but the others weren't so cooperative. RCA operators weren't responding quickly when asked by village telephone attendants for time and charges. Attendants tried to collect long-distance charges from callers at the time of call, but they couldn't collect from callers without the call information. RCA's long-dis-tance operators weren't helping.

And there was another problem. When village telephones were out of service because of RCA's technical problems, the local tele-phone company in Bethel, which did the billing on behalf of RCA, continued to charge the village for service. There was poor communication between RCA and the local company.

On top of it all, the villages in the Bethel area were being auto-matically charged a two percent Bethel city sales tax. But the villages themselves were far outside the Bethel city limits and clearly outside Bethel's jurisdiction.

These were all problems I had previously reported, but RCA had made no effort to solve them. They were threatening the success of the bush telephone program. I was concerned. RCA needed to get serious about making the program a success.

I often called headquarters to report these problems, but my calls weren't working. In December I decided to send them a memo. I was only a field supervisor, and they didn't expect a memo from me, but, nevertheless, I started my memo by saying:

> In several of the villages where we now have telephones in service, RCA's public image is terrible! Due to our failure to make certain critical arrangements, these villages have had difficulty paying their telephone bills, and this has resulted in telephones being disconnected (for nonpayment), interpersonal conflicts in the villages, and in generally bad public relations for RCA.[1]

I went on to describe the long-distance billing problems and how they had been resolved. Then I moved to the remaining problems. I explained that long-distance operators were not responding quickly when asked for charges. Village telephone attendants were waiting for hours to receive the long distance charges.

I'm sure they didn't expect such a comment from a field supervisor, but I called the situation "unacceptable." With such long delays, telephone attendants were finding it difficult or impossible to collect money from callers.

Then I described another problem:

"[When] a village telephone is out of service for a long period of time, the local telephone company continues to charge the village for service. Arrangements should be made with the local companies so that the villages' bills are adjusted for outages."[2]

And the other problem:

"Villages in the Bethel area are charged a 2% city sales tax. This is a City of Bethel tax, and does not pertain to the villages, which are outside the city limits."[3]

I concluded the memo by returning to the public relations theme:

"The problems described above are negatively affecting our image in the villages. I strongly suggest that Engineering, Plant, Marketing and Public Relations work together to correct them."[4]

I had done what I could to resolve these issues. It was time to go back to my real job, installing the radio phone system and making it work.

The high winds along Alaska's coast had blown down our antenna at the Cape Romanzof Air Force station. On the day after Christmas, John flew three of us — Terry McMahon, a new technician on our team, Denver Carney, an ironworker, and me — to Cape Romanzof, a remote U.S. Air Force station on the Bering Sea coast. The station's radar looked west to keep an eye on the Soviets, especially the Bear bombers and MiG fighters that sometimes lurked too close to the Alaska mainland. When they did, U.S. Air Force fighters scrambled from Alaska's Air Force bases to help them find their way back to the Soviet mainland.

Terry was a soft-spoken technician. We had worked together building a radio station a few years earlier. Terry was a good, steady worker and a man of few words.

But Denver was far from quiet, and he had many talents. An accomplished pilot, he owned his own Cessna 185, which, except for its yellow paint job with green trim, looked like a clone of our plane. The son of an Irish family, he grew up in Seattle, rough and ready, in the heart of the city's port area. A great ironworker, Denver could weld or bolt just about anything together, including antennas and towers. Denver talked as he worked. His running commentary let everyone know he was there.

The Air Force had allowed RCA to put a VHF base station at Cape Romanzof to link to radio phones in the nearby villages of Scammon Bay, Hooper Bay, and Chevak. Big, curved UHF antennas — they looked like old drive-in theater movie screens — connected the three villages' calls to Alaska's telephone network.[5]

The remote Cape Romanzof Air Force Station had two camps. The lower one was a base camp with an airstrip, and that's where John landed the Cessna. The wind screamed at base camp, but its weather was tame compared to top camp, where the radars and our radio gear were located.

We climbed aboard the station's "tram," a wooden platform 10 feet on a side with a flimsy-looking railing around its edge. The tram was suspended from a motor-driven steel cable. As John flew back to Bethel to keep the airplane safe, three of us crouched on the platform that carried us to top camp, and that's where we stayed for the next ten days.

Our big antenna array, four stacked antennas mounted on a heavy pipe we used as a mast, collected ice — lots of it. The ice increased the surface area of the antenna and mast, acting like a huge sail and increasing the wind's force on the structure. The antenna array had blown down, and we meant to fix it.

We planned to strengthen the antenna structure. I had shipped in heavy 4-inch pipe to use as a mast and thick 3/16-inch guy wire to replace the smaller pipe and wire that had first been used. The earlier structure just wasn't strong enough to withstand those Cape Romanzof winds.

But soon after we reached top camp, the wind picked up to more than 60 miles an hour. We could see that it would take us a while to do what was supposed to be a simple job, and we spent most of the next week inside waiting for the wind to back off.

Even after we finished installing the new, stronger antenna structure, high winds prevented us from leaving the mountain. The tram was our only way from the high radar station to the airstrip down at base camp. Concerned about safety, the Air Force ran the tram up and down the mountain only when the wind speed was below 30 miles an hour. So we waited a few more days.

We "celebrated" New Year's by turning in early at top camp. Finally, we took the tram down to base camp and flew back to Bethel with John on January 5. We had been on the mountain ten days to do what was supposed to be a one day job.

We were often weathered in that winter, and, even when we weren't weathered in, the Alaskan nights were long. John and I shared a hotel room at Bethel's Kuskokwim Inn, and it could be a raucous place. Excitement emanated from the Kashim Room, the bar next door. Bethel later became a "dry" town, where alcoholic beverages were banned, but then it was pretty "wet."

Sometimes it seemed that most of the excitement was focused outside our hotel room door. John slept with a loaded .357 Magnum pistol under his pillow, ready to stop any reveler who tried to enter. It made me a little nervous, though. My bed was between John's bed and the door.

We had lots of time to talk. Copies of *Time* magazine reached Bethel a week or so after they were delivered to the rest of the country, and we kept up on the news. We knew what was going on in the smaller states down south. The Watergate scandal was emerging. We read that John Dean had declared there was "a cancer on the presidency." We both suspected the worst about Watergate, but it wasn't until several months later that the worst was finally revealed.

John and I drank coffee as we waited for better flying weather. We talked about the problems confronting the bush telephone program. With the deadline for installation of 142 village phones only a year away and fewer than 25 phones in service, it was pretty clear that we wouldn't complete the project on time. It wasn't even close. I was becoming suspicious that RCA didn't have serious intentions to complete the project. I thought the company was just trying to put on a show to convince state officials they were trying.

The instructions we got from headquarters asked us to keep records that would later show that we had made an effort and that weather delays and other problems weren't the company's fault. To me it sounded like CYA. But John didn't share my skepticism.

"Don't sweat it," he said. "Just go with the flow."

Yet we both knew there was a bigger problem confronting us — connecting villages that were far from regional telephone centers and Air Force stations like Cape Romanzof. There were many villages along the Yukon and Kuskokwim rivers whose VHF radio phones would work only if their signals were relayed to Bethel by another system. RCA planned to build a string of mountaintop microwave relay stations to serve these villages.

But building and maintaining those stations looked to John and me like a big challenge. Alaska's worst weather hammered those mountaintops. Helicopters would need to fly in high winds to move men, equipment and fuel for the generators needed to power the mountaintop sites. Considering the problems we were already facing, the microwave relay stations looked like a dicey deal.

I had thought about putting satellite earth stations in the villages. Satellite earth stations are the ground systems needed to communicate with satellites in the sky. Referring to their dish-shaped antennas, some called the earth stations "satellite dishes." Earth stations could communicate through a satellite directly to Bethel or even to Anchorage, without any need for microwave relay stations.

"You know, satellites would probably be a better way to link the villages together," I said.

"How would that work?" John asked.

"With satellites, you need equipment only at the end points of a link. The relay station is the satellite in the sky. There's no need for mountaintop microwave stations," I explained.

In 1972 satellite earth stations were big and expensive. But technology advances could soon change that. It was possible that smaller, less expensive earth stations would soon be available. At least it seemed to be worth exploring.

I didn't know it then, but there were other Alaskans with the same idea.

4

ANCHORAGE

NOVEMBER 1972

As I spent November days working in Alaska's villages, Augie Hiebert sat in Anchorage surrounded by stacks of paper. He worked in the corner office of the same building that housed his three Anchorage broadcast stations. The building itself squatted in the middle of a field under the tall tower that held the stations' antennas. Augie was the CEO of Northern Television. The company owned five broadcast stations, the three Anchorage stations and two more in Fairbanks.

I hadn't yet met Augie, but I had certainly heard of him. He was an Alaska broadcasting legend. Years earlier, in 1939, Augie had come to Alaska to help build the first radio station in Fairbanks. Then he went on to create a small broadcasting empire. Slowly and patiently, he built first one station and then another.

But Augie was also passionate about public service. After he saw that first radio station's impact on the citizens of Fairbanks, he became a fierce advocate for more and better communication services across Alaska — and not just services that made a profit. He was a broadcast engineer and executive, but at heart Augie was a public servant.

As he worked in his office, Augie was planning a way to improve Alaska's telecommunication system.

In December 1916 August G. Hiebert was born in the fertile Columbia River Valley of eastern Washington. As a child he suffered a series of illnesses and injuries, but he still did well in school. A quiet and serious student, he graduated in 1935 first among a high school class of eight.[1]

Even before his high school graduation, when he was only 15, Augie qualified for his first ham radio license, earning the call letters W7CBF. Soon he had his own "ham shack" behind the family farmhouse. As a ham radio operator, Augie built his own radio equipment, and he learned and perfected his skills sending and receiving international Morse code.

Morse code was the best way to transmit when static and noise made reception difficult. It was better than voice communication because it was often possible, by using electronic tricks and a radio operator's sensitive ear, to get a message through. A Morse code signal could punch through difficult radio conditions.

To learn the code, Augie worked with a friend, hooking up tone generators to a telephone party line to send Morse code back and forth. It helped both of them hone their Morse code skills, increasing their code speed. But others on the party line weren't happy about listening to the transmissions. Soon the boys were banned from the phone line, so they connected their tone generators to a convenient barbed wire fence instead of the party line.[2]

But copying Morse code was just part of the challenge of being a "radio ham." It was part of the radio tradition. For years other radio operators had done the same, sending and receiving important messages in times of war and peace. As a teenager Augie was continuing the tradition of many radio operators who had come before him.

After Augie's high school graduation, his grandfather recognized his interest in electronics and enrolled him in an electronics course. At first he took the course by correspondence, but he later traveled to Los Angeles to finish the last few months of the course.[3]

Augie was learning the fundamentals of radio, which he knew could lead to gainful employment. But radio would later become even more important for him

In 1939, when he was only 22, Augie had what must have seemed like the opportunity of a lifetime. He was asked to travel from the Pacific Northwest to Fairbanks, Alaska to help build a new radio station. Its call letters would be KFAR. The station was backed by Austin E. (Capt) Lathrop, a rough and ready, but wealthy, boat captain and entrepreneur who had been persuaded to build the first radio station in Fairbanks. Augie arrived there in August 1939.[4]

Augie worked with another young engineer, Stan Bennett, the station's chief engineer, even though he was only a few years older than Augie. They soon finished building KFAR, and the station went on the air on October 1, 1939. At 610 on the AM dial, the station's power was only 1000 watts, but it was enough to provide a new and needed service to Fairbanks and the sur-rounding area.[5]

KFAR needed a way to receive news of the outside world for broadcast to Fairbanks listeners. But there were no computers, and KFAR had no teletype service in those early days. Augie and Stan needed a reliable system to receive the news.

The two young engineers found a way. They built two huge shortwave antennas. The long wires were set up in the shape of a four-sided *rhombus*.[6] Each *rhombic* antenna was 850 feet long with four long wires strung between telephone poles. One antenna was pointed toward New York and the other toward San Francisco. The shortwave Morse code transmissions came from a primary station in New York, but when radio conditions between New York and Fairbanks weren't favorable, San Francisco was the backup.

4-1 Young Augie Hiebert spoke to KFAR listeners as his dog Sparky listened attentively.

The two antenna system was reliable. Stan and Augie spent hours each day "copying press." The transmissions came via Morse code at a blistering 40 to 50 words per minute. That was fast, even for an experienced ham operator like Augie. But the system worked, and KFAR listeners stayed up-to-date on world and national news.[7]

Capt Lathrop had a hands-off approach in running the station. He just hired capable young people like Augie and Stan and let them take care of things. He saw the station as a public service that he was providing to Fairbanks. That spirit of public service made an impression on the young Augie Hiebert.

Augie's daughter Robin Chlupach later wrote:

> Capt did not seem to be concerned whether the radio station was a money-making proposition. The venture for him was philanthropic. He selected an experienced and capable staff, provided the environment for them to work effectively, and then left them alone to do the job. Working for Capt was an unequalled opportunity. The staff at KFAR was free to produce a diversity of programming to meet the needs of the community and to fill the void in communications. That versatility was exemplary of a bygone era.[8]

The communication system in Alaska was pretty limited in those days. In fact, there wasn't much communication service at all. But KFAR filled the gap with a daily program called "Tundra Topics." It was a one-way message service. Each day the station sent out messages submitted by listeners.

A message delivered to the station was read on the air with the hope that it would be picked up by its intended recipient. The same kind of service was replicated by many other Alaska radio stations in the decades that followed. Other stations later used other names for the service, names like: "Caribou Clatter," "Village Hotline," and "Tundra Telegraph." But the service was always the same.[9]

Major league baseball was popular across America, and Fairbanks was no exception. Baseball was, after all, the national pastime. The Fairbanks teams' games were broadcast live, but major league baseball, including the World Series, was a different story. KFAR carried what they called "live" broadcasts of major league games. Announcer and station manager Bud Foster did the play-by-play based on sparse information.[10]

There was a special communication relay system that worked through the military-operated Alaska Communications System — the ACS. Using special abbreviations, 25 words or so for each inning would arrive by telegraph at the ACS station, and a runner would carry the telegram over to KFAR and deliver it to Bud. From this sparse information, Bud created the play-by-play for the entire inning. And he used sound effects. A pencil striking a piece of wood was the crack of the bat. A pencil striking a roll of toilet paper was the sound of the ball hitting the catcher's mitt. The sounds created the illusion that the listener was tuned to a broadcast coming directly from the ballpark.[11]

On the morning of Sunday, December 7, 1941, Augie was relaxing at the station and listening to a drama on a shortwave receiver. Soon he heard an announcer interrupt the shortwave broadcast, saying "Japanese planes are bombing Honolulu, have attacked Pearl Harbor, and are bombing Hickam Field." Augie was the first person in Alaska to hear the news. He phoned the military commander at Ladd Field in Fairbanks. The base commander, previously unaware of the attack, contacted the commanding general of the Alaska Defense Command at Fort Richardson in Anchorage, who also hadn't heard about the attack. And that's how Alaska's military leaders first received the news that Pearl Harbor had been bombed. Two hours later they were notified through official channels.[12]

Many years later Augie's company owned and operated five radio and television stations in Anchorage and Fairbanks. Augie's passion was building and improving Alaska's communication systems to provide better service to Alaskans — whether or not he made money doing it. He had learned about public service from Capt Lathrop.

In 1961 Augie first saw the potential of satellite communication technology for Alaska. That was the year Alaska was visited by the famous rocket and missile scientist Dr. Wernher Von Braun, then the director of the National Aeronautics and Space Administration (NASA). Augie escorted Von Braun around the state — to Fairbanks to visit the University of Alaska and to Point Barrow to visit the National Arctic Research Laboratory. From Barrow they were flown by helicopter to a U.S. Coast Guard icebreaker operating in the Arctic Ocean. The two men spent lots of time together. They had time to talk.[13]

Von Braun told Augie how earth-orbiting satellites could provide communication service anywhere on earth. That was when Augie began to think seriously about satellite communication technology. A few years later, in the summer of 1964, he announced that his company Northern Television had acquired shares in the Communications Satellite Corporation — COMSAT. The purchase was announced as a front-page story in the Anchorage Daily Times on July 6, 1964. But Augie wasn't seeking financial profit. He saw the purchase of the COMSAT shares as an investment in Alaska's future.[14]

Later in 1964 Augie helped to found the new Alaska Broadcasters Association (ABA), and he became its first president. At the time Augie's vision for the association was to promote satellite communication technology for use in Alaska.[15]

At every opportunity in the years that followed, Augie promoted the idea that satellite communication technology should be an important part of Alaska's future. He pushed, and then he pushed some more, talking to Alaska's governor, other public officials, COMSAT, and anyone else who would listen.

Augie wouldn't be happy until Alaska had its own satellite earth station.

In 1968 COMSAT approved the construction of a new earth station near Talkeetna, and Gov. Walter J Hickel announced in April 1968 that Augie would chair a seven member satellite communication task force to coordinate the state's efforts with COMSAT.

The new satellite earth station would be linked to an Intelsat communication satellite located over the Pacific, and the new link would connect Alaska with the "South 48," Hawaii, Japan, the South Pacific and the world beyond. By 1969 the earth station was under construction. Even before its completion, Augie proposed that it be named the Bartlett Earth Station after U.S. Senator Bob Bartlett, who had been a key to obtaining COMSAT's commitment to build the station. Senator Bartlett had recently passed away.[16]

Augie's daughter Robin Chlupach wrote in her book *Airwaves Over Alaska*:

> The Bartlett Earth Station, the farthest north of its kind in the satellite communication system, was one of eight similar facilities in the United States. The huge dish, 98 feet in diameter, sitting atop a 16-foot concrete pedestal is still a breathtaking site. The pedestal serves as the control facility for the operation. The antenna structure, standing the height of a 10 story building and weighing 315 tons, can be rotated rapidly at 1° per second, and precisely track within 2/100 of a degree, a satellite stationed at 22,300 miles altitude.[17]

4-2 The Bartlett earth station was built near Talkeetna.

July 21, 1969 was a historic day for Alaska, the nation and the world. Even though the new earth station was still under construction, it was pressed into service early to give Alaska a live look at a big event. It was the day that Neil Armstrong set foot on the moon.

The moon landing was broadcast on Augie's Anchorage television station KTVA-TV. But, with his usual devotion to public service, Augie made sure that the program was also available to his competitors, the two other Anchorage television stations. Augie coordinated the hookup for all three stations. Alaska received its first live television broadcast on that day. Almost a year later, on June 30, 1970, the big earth station was officially dedicated and named the Bartlett Earth Station in honor of U.S. Senator Bob Bartlett.[18]

The Bartlett earth station was huge, and it was expensive. It didn't seem economical or possible to build satellite earth stations in other parts of Alaska.

But that would soon change.

5

FAIRBANKS

MARCH 1973

At about the same time John and I were in Bethel, drinking coffee and waiting for better flying weather, Professor Bob Merritt worked in his antenna lab in Fairbanks. The lab was in the engineering building on the University of Alaska campus. Surrounded by a cluster of eager engineering students, Bob used a soldering iron and a spool of solder to connect a transmission line to the *yagi* antenna he had just built. It looked something like one of the television antennas installed above the rooftops of nearby homes.

As he worked, Bob answered the questions of curious students.

"How does this piece work?"

"Why isn't it connected to the transmission line?"

The patient professor thoughtfully responded to all the questions.

Soon the soldering job was complete, and Bob asked the students to try out the new antenna, testing it on a short communication link from one end of the lab to the other.

When the test was complete, Bob suggested, "Why don't you take it outside and give it a try?"

The young students knew they were in the presence of a master.

Robert Merritt was born in 1924 and grew up in Oregon. He graduated from Oregon State College in 1949 and six years later landed in Fairbanks Alaska, where he took a job as a junior faculty member at the University of Alaska.

Bob soon became an expert in two fields of electrical engineering. One was power engineering, with its heavy machinery and the big lines needed for the transmission of electrical energy. But Bob also became an expert in radio engineering. He knew about receivers, transmitters and, most important in Alaska, the behavior of radio waves. He learned how and why the waves travel over short and long distances, and, in each situation, which frequencies and antennas would work best.

5-1 Professor Bob Merritt in his University of Alaska laboratory.

With his dark rimmed glasses and rumpled white shirt, Bob looked like a stereotypical engineer. His shirt's pocket protector bulged with a rainbow of colored pens. Revered by his colleagues as a "dirty-handed engineer," Bob could build just about anything — and then make it work.

Years earlier in 1945, science fiction writer Arthur C. Clarke suggested that artificial earth satellites, orbiting high above the earth, could pick up and retransmit signals from the ground, making communication over very long distances possible without the need for ground-based facilities, except those at a communication link's end points.

It was something like ham operators talking with friends in foreign lands by bouncing shortwave signals off the ionosphere. But conditions in the ionosphere varied, and the shortwave bounce was fickle. Satellite connections would be steady and reliable.

Eight years after his arrival in Fairbanks, Bob Merritt helped his students experience a landmark event in the new field of satellite communications. It was October 4, 1957, and the Soviets had just launched Sputnik.

The new satellite emitted a "beep-beep" signal on shortwave. Working with his colleague Glenn Stanley, Bob scrambled to rig up some receiving equipment. They tuned in the radio transmissions from Sputnik, and surrounded by students, Bob and Glenn heard and recorded Sputnik's "beep beep" on a big tape machine. It was the first artificial earth orbiting satellite capable of sending out a radio signal.

At the time Bob and Glenn may not have foreseen what Sputnik represented for Alaska's telecommunication future.

That would soon change.

5-2 Professors Bob Merritt (left) and Glenn Stanley (right) helped engineering students tune in transmissions from Sputnik in October 1957.

Health care in Alaska villages was provided by specially trained village health aides, and they were critically dependent on shortwave communication. At least once a day, each region's health aides kept a "radio schedule" to talk with a doctor in the region's hospital. The villages in the interior part of Alaska, where the university was located, depended on doctors at the hospital in the village of Tanana.

The health aides used radio to describe a patient's symptoms and their own observations. Doctors advised the health aides on how to care for patients, in some cases prescribing medications available in the health aides' well-supplied medicine cabinets.

The weak link in this system was shortwave radio. When the *aurora borealis* — the northern lights — was active, shortwave

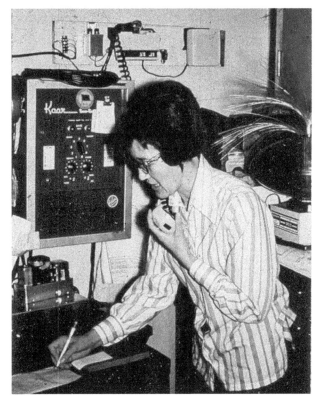

5-3 A village health aide consulted with a doctor using shortwave radio.

communication could be cut off for days at a time. Village patients were the victims.

Beginning in 1966 NASA launched a series of experimental satellites. NASA called it the Applied Technology Satellite — or ATS — project. Over the next eight years NASA launched satellites designated ATS-1 through ATS-6. The first and last of these were used to conduct experiments and demonstrations in Alaska.[1]

ATS-1 was launched in 1966, and NASA positioned it over the Pacific Ocean, where it covered Alaska and a number of Pacific islands. Bob Merritt and Glenn Stanley worked on a project aimed at using ATS-1 to improve the communication system used by village health aides.[2]

The ATS-1 satellite used VHF radio, far less sensitive than short-wave to atmospheric conditions. To build an experimental health aide communication system, Bob used 100-watt taxicab radios. They were cheap and readily available. The radios needed some modification, which Bob carried out easily. And he designed a special antenna that could be built cheaply and easily installed in some Alaska villages. It was a great project for a dirty handed engineer.

Bob and his students built the specially designed antennas. They were a sight to behold. There was a helix, a corkscrew shaped element that pointed directly at the ATS-1 satellite. The corkscrew was backed by a hexagonal screen that reflected the waves and helped to direct them toward the satellite. One of the antennas could be used in a village to transmit signals up to the ATS-1 satellite and receive the signals coming down from the satellite.[3]

5-4 Bob Merritt's corkscrew antennas helped village health aides reliably communicate with doctors through the ATS-1 satellite.

The ATS-1 satellite demonstration project began in 1971. The VHF radios and Bob's antennas were installed in 26 locations. Most of them were villages but a few were larger towns. "Radio call," was conducted each day, just as it had been using shortwave. But the satellite communication system was reliable! The health aides loved it!

Yet the health aides were later disappointed because ATS-1 was just a temporary demonstration project. When the project ended, and the health aides went back to using their shortwave radios. Still, the appeal of using satellite communication technology to serve Alaska's villages had been proven.[4]

6

LITTLE DIOMEDE

APRIL 1973

We were airborne and headed into a contest with the wind.

Three of us were aboard the Cessna, and we were nearing the Inupiaq village of Ignaluk. We could see it nestled into the side of Alaska's Little Diomede Island, near the middle of the Bering Strait and separated by little more than two miles from Big Diomede Island, part of Russsia, which was in turn part of the Soviet Union. The international dateline and the Russia-U.S. border lay midway between the two islands.

The Cessna's landing gear was a wheel-ski combination — just right for conditions between the two Diomedes. But the sea ice was far from a glassy skating pond and didn't look great for a landing. Strong winds and currents had created huge heaps of snow-covered ice called "pressure ridges." Some were 20 to 30 feet high.

From our airborne Cessna, Little Diomede Island looked like a mesa sitting in a desert of saltwater ice. We could see its high, flat top and its steep sides plunging down to the frozen sea. Tucked at the base of the steep slope on the west side of the island,

Ignaluk faced the island's Russian brother, Big Diomede Island, across a jumble of sea ice. The big island was uninhabited except for a military observation post.

6-1 The sea ice on the island's west side was distorted by big pressure ridges. The village was off in the distance.

A villager later told me he sometimes trained a telescope on the Soviet outpost.

"What do you see?" I asked.

"A Soviet soldier looking back at me," was his answer.

The three aboard the Cessna were John, a technician and me. The technician and I would stay at Little Diomede until the job was done, but, with no safe place to tie down the Cessna, John would to go back to Nome and wait there until we were ready for a pickup.

But first he had to find a landing place on the sea ice that was free of the big pressure ridges. The village had no airstrip and could be reached by boat during the few months of summer when the Bering Strait was liquid or by air during the months of March and April, when there might be few ice patches smooth enough to land a small plane on skis.

John lined up on some ski tracks where another pilot had landed. The Cessna touched down. We came to a stop near the village, but John kept the plane's engine idling with the nose pointed into the wind. The airspeed indicator read almost 50 knots — about 50 miles an hour — indicating the wind's speed, not the plane's. With the wind screaming, we unloaded the equipment and tools we would need to install the radio phone and its antenna.[1]

John wasted no time heading back to Nome, leaving the two of us to start our work. Thinking that the wind would soon slow down, we began indoors, installing the radio phone equipment. The next day, with the wind still howling, we worked outside on frozen ground, putting together the big radio antenna and making it ready to be erected when the wind calmed down.

6-2 The village was built on the island's steep western slope.

But, on the third and fourth days, with the wind still unabated, I talked with village chief James Iyapanna and asked him when the wind would stop.

A man of few words, James said "wind never stop."

He told me that the previous year the Alaska National Guard had installed a "wind meter" at the village, but "it blew away." There was no need to say more.[2]

The same day, as we waited for the wind to subside, James was on the frozen sea ice west of the village. He was seal hunting with a rifle slung across his back. Visibility was bad because of the blowing snow, and surrounding pressure ridges sometimes blocked his view.

But James heard someone shouting and calling him by his Inupiaq name. He looked up to see a cousin who had lived on Big Diomede Island many years earlier. The two men whooped and hollered a joyous reunion on the sea ice somewhere near the international boundary, indistinct to the two men standing on rugged sea ice in blizzard conditions.[3]

For many years the villagers of Alaska's Little Diomede Island had no contact with their friends and relatives who had once lived on the big island. Shortly after the end of World War II, at the beginning of the Cold War, officials in a faraway Soviet city decided that the village on Big Diomede would be closed and the villagers relocated to the mainland. The Little Diomeders knew only that their friends had disappeared. It happened in 1947.[4]

But in 1973 things changed, at least for short time. It was the first contact between the people of the two Diomedes in 26 years.[5]

The two men agreed to meet at the same place on the sea ice the next day. This time each of them brought a group of their own villagers. The men of Ignaluk learned that their friends had been allowed by Soviet authorities to return to their island for a few weeks to do some hunting and trapping, but this small pleasure would be followed by a forced return to the Russian mainland. Nevertheless, it was a joyful reunion.[6]

The meetings continued for the next few days. Each night James showed me watches, cigarettes, and other Soviet goods — labeled of course, in Cyrillic letters — that they had received in trade. Alaskans knew very little about the Russian side of the Bering Sea. Though the far eastern part of Russia was very close to western Alaska, there had been virtually no communication across the Bering Sea for many years. But we were starting to learn a little of the mystery that took place behind the "ice curtain."[7]

I wanted to join the daily meetings, but James hesitated. He worried that he and his fellow villagers were violating a national or international law, and he assumed that having an outsider at the meetings could only make things worse.[8]

But later, after my return to mainland Alaska, word of the "international" meetings reached Nome and then the U.S. State Department in Washington, DC. The State Department's response was to deputize Nome mayor Leo Rasmussen. Leo flew out to Little Diomede, and, on behalf of the State Department, "blessed" the sea ice meetings that had taken place. James needn't have worried.[9]

Finally, after we had waited for four days, the wind slowed down — but not much. We decided to try to raise the antenna. It would have been impossible for our little two-man crew to do it alone, but the villagers, at ease working in the weather conditions, volunteered to help. They thought nothing of scrambling across icy rooftops in a gale. They tied ropes to the mast, and easily raised it to an upright position. Few words were spoken. We needed only to secure the guy wires and retreat to the warmth of the village school.[10]

A bystander would have said we pointed the big antenna the wrong way. It was pointed west —toward Russia — even though the Alaskan mainland was to the east. But, if we had pointed the antenna toward the mainland, its radio waves would have collided with the high cliffs behind the village with no hope of finding their target in Alaska.[11]

We didn't have the means to install an antenna on the island's flat tabletop, with its clear view to the east. Instead, we did the next best thing, aiming the antenna directly at the cliffs of Big Diomede, where it its signals were reflected back to the Alaska mainland. With the technician slowly turning the antenna, first right and then left, I watched the equipment's signal strength meter until we found an antenna position where our radio transmissions reflected perfectly off the big island's cliffs and, after twice crossing the international boundary, reached our radio base station on the mainland. The signal was strong and steady.[12]

Usually, when we designed radio phone installations, we tried to avoid reflected signals, which could cause problems when they combined with signals that had followed a direct path. But this time reflected signals were the solution — not the problem. They were the only way to establish a reliable radio link.[13]

I tested the telephone and it worked just fine. I called John in Nome to ask for a pickup. Then, as we waited, there was little to do but read books and listen to the howling wind. When John picked us up two days later, we had spent a week at Ignaluk, most of it waiting for the wind to accommodate raising our antenna or for the second landing of our plane.[14]

When John picked us up, we had some stories to tell.

I was an eager young engineer, and I was glad to be doing important work connecting Alaska's villages to each other and to the world beyond. Who could argue with providing villagers with a reliable telephone system that allowed urgently needed medical communication, calls to order snow machine parts, and calls to "Junior" attending high school hundreds or thousands of miles away? I had embarked on an adventure doing important work.

But I still had doubts about RCA's commitment to its bush telephone program.

We were two years into the program, and only 22 of 142 villages had operating telephones. My team was the only one working in the villages. It was pretty obvious that RCA wouldn't be able to meet its commitment to provide service to all of the villages within three years.

I received more messages from headquarters saying that it was most important to document the reasons phone service was not working. It didn't sound like an all-out push to get things working.

I made calls to headquarters and sent them a string of memos documenting existing problems and requesting assistance in resolving them. There was no response.

I wondered, *Do they think I'm just a troublemaker?*

When John and I talked about it, he again advised me to "just relax."

"Why don't you just go with the flow? This is just how things work in a big company like RCA. You're being an idealist," he said.

John was probably right — at least about the idealist part. But I wanted to get the phones working in as many villages as possible.

I understood that RCA shareholders expected the company to make a profit. But RCA had made a commitment. I thought that even a profit-oriented company should be obligated to put forth its best effort to keep a commitment regardless of the costs or difficulties it encountered.

Eventually, I decided that I could help the villages more by working outside the company. I submitted my resignation effective in May 1973, just a year after I had originally signed on with RCA.

A few weeks later I decided to write one last letter to RCA. This one went all the way to the top. It was addressed to Mr. Stephen Heller, the president and CEO of RCA Alaska Communications. In my letter I described the problems that I thought were holding back village phone service, and I asked the CEO to take action to correct the problem.

I was no longer a RCA employee, and I thought I could speak freely — even to the RCA Alascom CEO. I might be able to have a bigger impact on the success of the bush telephone program than I did as an employee working in the field.

I started my June 25 letter this way:

> Dear Mr. Heller:
>
> "RCA Alascom" is becoming a bad word in the bush. I would like to tell you why. This letter is an attempt to help you correct some of the problems RCA is having in the rural areas of the state.
>
> To explain my particular perspective, I spent the past year working as field installation supervisor on RCA's bush telephone project. In this position I became aware of several problem areas which required the attention of headquarters people. After making repeated unsuccessful efforts to have some of these problems corrected, I became convinced that the Alascom organization was unresponsive and ineffective. Disenchanted, I decided to resign and go on to other things, but, of course, my resignation did not help to improve communications in the bush. Perhaps this letter will."[15]

In my letter I described errors in the bills that General Telephone was sending to the villages. Villages had been receiving bills for long periods when their telephones were out of service because of RCA's technical problems, and they were not able to get RCA or General Telephone, Bethel's local telephone company, to correct the errors. There was also the Bethel sales tax problem, where villages were unreasonably being charged sales tax to be sent to a community many miles away. I asked if RCA had "abdicated its responsibility to village customers" by having General Telephone do the billing.[16]

Emphasizing that villagers were trying to make good on their end of their bargain with RCA, I said:

> It's ironic that the villagers are usually correct in their local bookkeeping procedures, but the men with computers and sophisticated accounting techniques continue to make mistakes.[17]

And that left the biggest problem of all, the very slow progress of the bush telephone program:

> It is becoming increasingly clear that RCA will not be able to meet announced completion dates for village telephone service. Only 22 Phase I villages have service, and Phase II installation hasn't even started yet.[18]

Returning to RCA's credibility issue, I said:

> What counts is not what you say, but what you do. The people are due explanations of the delays and realistic estimates of when they can expect telephone service[19]

But I tried to end on a conciliatory note, writing:

> This letter is not intended to be vindictive... On the contrary, I hope it will be helpful to you in

improving Alascom service to the bush. A service orientation seems to be absent from the company right now, but I think that can be changed, and an organization which is both responsive and effective could be the result.[20]

I didn't know that the letter would be the beginning of a year-long correspondence with the RCA Alascom CEO.

7

KOTZEBUE

NOVEMBER 1973

The Arctic wind stung my face. The feeling was more pain than cold. I steered the snow machine[1] into the early morning darkness and turned onto the snow-covered tundra, pointing the machine away from town.

The snow seemed brushed with a broom, piling up in the eddy behind every object that disturbed the wind's path. Blowing snow hid the transmitter building that perched near an invisible coastline. With the sea frozen, snow covered both sea ice and tundra, blending them and obscuring the boundary between land and sea. The Arctic in winter was a moonscape on earth.

Public radio station KOTZ served Inupiaq communities spread along the rivers and coasts of northwest Alaska. Its studios were tucked into the schoolhouse in Kotzebue, a small cluster of buildings huddled on a gravel spit jutting into the Chukchi Sea. For centuries Kotzebue's people had subsisted on the beluga whale, bearded seal and ring seal they took from the sea and the caribou they hunted on land.

The town was 30 miles north of the Arctic Circle. Its small, wood frame houses had replaced the traditional sod huts that once squatted on the gravel spit. I was headed away from Kotzebue toward the transmitter building, less than a mile from town but with no winter road. I needed to check that things were operating properly — part of my work as manager and engineer.

I wore multiple layers to blunt the wind's chill. The layers were topped by insulated snow pants, Inupiaq-made boots of caribou hide, down-filled mittens, and a parka with a hood trimmed in wolf fur. A knitted balaclava covered my head and face except where my eyes peered through a narrow slit that was covered by goggles. Exposed flesh would freeze in less than a minute.

Coastal Kotzebue had milder weather than the Arctic interior, where winter temperatures could plunge to 60 degrees below zero Fahrenheit and winds could cause chill temperatures to minus 100 degrees. But in Kotzebue temperatures rarely dropped below minus 30 degrees. The wind compensated though. Wind speeds up to 30 or 40 miles per hour could drive chill temperatures to 100 below zero, equaling those found in the interior.

I opened the door to the small transmitter building, and warm, soothing air rushed over me. I shook the snow from my parka and, once inside, stood under the electric space heater. The 5000-watt radio transmitter should have made enough heat to warm such a small building, but this was the Arctic, and the space heater gave an extra boost.

As my body thawed, I shed my parka and mittens and began to work. The building's bare, white walls surrounded my toolbox and four racks of equipment. In three of the racks, unadorned gray door panels covered the innards of the 5000-watt transmitter that pushed the KOTZ signal out to northwest Alaska. Only a row of meters was visible across the transmitter's upper edge. I opened the gray panels, exposing an array of knobs and smaller meters that I would use to make adjustments. The fourth rack of

7-1 I drove to the KOTZ transmitter aboard this snow machine, my usual transportation in Kotzebue.

equipment held the meters and dials that were part of the studio-to-transmitter radio link and remote control system that allowed the transmitter to be controlled from our schoolhouse studio. The equipment radiated heat and the smell of dust.

My work was minor, and I would soon be back in the biting wind. I needed only to read a few meters and turn a few knobs to make minor adjustments. But when more serious technical problems arose, I would peel off layers of warm clothes and settle in to do needed repairs. I sometimes plugged in a soldering iron and used it to install new parts, with the smell of the solder's rosin and a curl of smoke in my face.

Marvin Weatherly had introduced me to KOTZ — and public radio — in May 1973. I met him just as I bottomed out in my disillusionment with RCA's bush telephone program.

We connected right away. Marv had been a U.S. Marine in the Korean War. He had come ashore with the First Marine Division in the famous 1950 Inchon invasion. I later served in the Army in Korea, and I knew the spot at Inchon where Marv and his fellow Marines had landed 17 years before my own military service.

After his time in the Marines, Marv worked in Alaska, including a job with Northern Television, Augie Hiebert's company. Working for Augie in 1960, Marv stumbled into the role of first announcer on Augie's new Anchorage radio station KTVA-FM, the first FM station in Alaska. Marv was working as an engineer but, for the station's first transmissions, he was temporarily pressed into service as an announcer.[2]

After another stint in Vietnam as a civilian working for military contractors, Marv returned to Alaska, and in 1970 he took a job as chief engineer for Augie's radio and television stations in Fairbanks. Then, in 1972, Marv became the chief engineer and assistant director of the Alaska Educational Broadcasting Commission — the AEBC — the state agency established in 1970 to deliver public broadcast service to unserved parts of the state.

Rural Alaska — those vast expanses dotted by small villages — generally had no broadcast service at all. Villagers could only hope that a signal from an AM station in a distant city would "skip" in at night, bringing music and news for an hour or two. There were few local stations. That's why Alaska's state government created the AEBC and provided some money to start a chain of public radio stations across rural Alaska.

Marv had heard about my work on the bush telephone project, and he called me on the phone.

"I hear that RCA is dragging its feet," he said.

"That's an understatement," I answered.

But Marv quickly jumped to a problem that concerned him more — the absence of an engineer at Kotzebue's new public radio station KOTZ.

Money was tight for Alaska's public radio stations, and there wasn't enough to hire both a general manager and a chief engineer for each station. Engineers were harder to find than managers. AEBC's solution: recruit an engineer and then tell him, "By the way, you're also the station manager."

Marv really wanted to find an engineer. He had been filling in temporarily, commuting from Anchorage to Kotzebue, 550 air miles each way, to do maintenance and take care of other engineering work. He was tired of it.

And Marv knew that I loved rural Alaska. Living and working in Kotzebue wouldn't be a problem for me. When he asked me to take the job, we agreed that I would give him an answer after making a visit to the new station.

A crusty Alaskan later helped me make the decision.

The jet engines' whine dropped as the Alaska Airlines 727 pilot throttled back and began the descent into Kotzebue. From the air I could see the town sitting on a gravel spit. It was late June 1973, and the summer Arctic sun shone, as it did around the clock. I stepped off the jet and saw my hosts waiting for me.

The short, wiry Ed Ward had a three-day stubble and a straight-talking style. He'd been in the Alaska bush for a long time, and, after I heard him speak, I knew he was also a radio guy. But I didn't yet know about Ed's remarkable past.

His daughter, the 18-year old Nellie Ward, was bubbly. She had started work as an announcer at KOTZ, and she was thrilled to be on the staff.

7-2 From the air I could see Kotzebue sitting on a gravel spit.

Ed squinted at me with a critical eye. As I spoke, he sized me up.

Then as we walked around the small town and toured the radio station's studio, Ed did most of the talking.

After a time he said "I like you, boy."

And he added a command.

"Take the job."

Two weeks later I packed my meager possessions and moved to Kotzebue.

8

KOTZEBUE

NOVEMBER 1973

After making adjustments to the transmitter, I locked the small building, remounted the snow machine, and pulled its starter cord. With the engine running, I turned toward the KOTZ studio to get ready for the station's morning sign-on. It was 5:30 AM, still long before the 11:00 AM winter sunrise. The village's twisting streets were quiet. But, after the 6 AM sign-on, Kotzebue would begin to come alive.

Leaving the cold again, I entered the warmth of Kotzebue's only school, loping down the stairs to our basement studios to begin preparations for the broadcast day. A year earlier, because no other space was available, the studios and office had been built in the basement of the school. Even with heating pipes crisscrossing overhead, the station was functional and comfortable.

We had two studios, an office, and a lobby we used for receiving visitors and socializing. There were no outside windows, but interior windows were many. It was, after all, a radio station. Later in the day those windows would reveal frenetic activity inside the station's nerve center. A visitor's eyes would be drawn to the busy studios and the announcers spinning records, twirling dials, and doing on-air interviews.

KOTZ was one of a new breed of radio stations that had started to pop up in America in the late 1960s. Public radio stations were meant to be alternatives to the commercial stations that provided service to most of the United States. The commercial stations often didn't provide programming that appealed to certain small audiences. People who enjoyed classical music, folk music or jazz were examples. The thinking was that commercial stations had no economic incentives to serve such small numbers of people and that, as long as they were supported by advertising, things wouldn't change. So public radio was born.

But we were different. KOTZ, while officially a public radio station with no advertising support, didn't fit the pattern. In fact, a few of the nation's mainstream public broadcasters were horrified to hear that there was a public radio station in Alaska that was playing Top 40 and country music.

But our listeners were happy, and I was happy. We were meeting an important need. There were no commercial stations serving northwest Alaska, and there was no prospect for advertiser-supported radio in such a remote part of the state. The same was true in other rural parts of Alaska. That's why Alaskan public radio stations, with music like ours and some unique local programs, were started — with state support — in the early 1970s.

The first rural Alaska public radio station was Bethel's KYUK, which began broadcasting in the summer of 1971. Next was Kotzebue's KOTZ, which signed on in April 1973, just a few months before I arrived.

Unlike other public radio stations of the day —mostly FM stations — KOTZ was on the AM band, the one usually frequented by commercial stations. That was because of the greater reach of an AM signal. We were only a 5000-watt station, but our listening area was huge, covering far more than 50,000 square miles.

Our AM frequency allowed our signal to be picked up in all of the villages across northwest Alaska.

Whether they listened on a portable, battery-operated radio while fishing for salmon in the summer, or huddled near a cabin's wood stove late on a winter night, our regular listeners received steady, reliable signals. But KOTZ also reached more distant listeners. Our nighttime signals skipped to Russia, Japan and other countries in Asia, and we sometimes received letters and postcards from listeners in these faraway places.

My first task in the morning was to make coffee. Next was our teletype machine, the electromechanical contraption that connected us to the Associated Press wire service, the source of our state, national and international news. But the teletype machine was a technological relic. Sitting on the floor in the corner of our reception area and standing waist high, the machine clackety-clacked as it typed out the news of the day relayed from distant cities of the nation and the world. The wire service "copy" would later be ready for our announcers to "rip and read" the day's news to KOTZ listeners.

Teletype was an early form of digital technology. Teletype messages were sent as a series of current pulses. Today's computer geeks might call them "ones" and "zeros." Just as a modern computer interprets a certain pattern of ones and zeros as an "A," a teletype machine interpreted a particular pattern of current pulses as an "A." The teletype patterns were different from those used by today's computers, but the idea was the same.

Translating the pulses into written text needed a complex jumble of mechanical and electromechanical parts. Together they clicked and clacked in a recognizable cacophony that told me the teletype was working properly. The machine's complexity included relays, gears, arms and levers, all needing my tender care to keep them adjusted, oiled and working properly.

But my early-morning task was simpler — just to change the machine's paper and ribbon. We kept rolls of teletype paper to satisfy the machine's voracious appetite. The ribbon — similar to the typewriter ribbons of the day — had to be changed often, a familiar chore to engineers and announcers working in radio stations in the 1970s and earlier.

With the coffee pot perking and the teletype machine resupplied, it was time for sign-on. In the studio I pushed a few buttons, and the remote-control equipment activated the transmitter in its small building on the snow-swept tundra. Pushing another button started our recorded sign-on and the broadcast day.

The sign-on tape began with the "Alaska Flag Song." It was Alaska's national anthem.

> *Eight stars of gold on a field of blue —*
>
> *Alaska's flag. May it mean to you*
>
> *The blue of the sea, the evening sky,*
>
> *The mountain lakes, and the flow'rs nearby;*
>
> *The gold of the early sourdough dreams,*
>
> *The precious gold of the hills and streams;*
>
> *The brilliant stars in the northern sky,*
>
> *The "Bear" — the "Dipper" — and, shining high,*
>
> *The great North Star with its steady light,*
>
> *Over land and sea a beacon bright.*
>
> *Alaska's flag — to Alaskans dear,*
>
> *The simple flag of a last frontier.*

The words and music were well-known to every school child and nearly every adult Alaskan from Arctic villages to the far away cities of Anchorage and Fairbanks. The song and its namesake flag bound Alaska's peoples together. Most Alaskans knew the words of their state song by memory, and they revered the flag's "eight stars of gold on a field of blue." The eight stars are the most prominent ones in the northern sky, the Big Dipper — also called the Great Bear — and the North Star.

8-1 Alaska's state flag, featuring two icons of the northern sky, the Big Dipper and the North Star.

Next came the pre-recorded voice of young Joe Hill, one of our staff announcers. He made the familiar sign-on announcement: "Welcome to another day of broadcasting here at KOTZ…Owned and operated by Kotzebue Broadcasting Incorporated, KOTZ uses a frequency of 720 kilohertz at a power of 5000 watts, as authorized by the Federal Communications Commission…" The FCC might have raised an eyebrow if it had known about *all* of our operating practices, but, until the commission ordered otherwise, we continued to serve our devoted listeners.

With the sign-on complete, it was time for the "Alex in the Morning" radio show. I was, by this time, wide awake, and my job was to help listeners start the day. The show began with upbeat banjo theme music, followed by a voice-over. "Good morning northwest Alaska! Hello Kiana! How ya doin', Shungnak," I said, naming two of the villages in our listening area. The morning news, weather forecasts, and a blend of Top 40 and country music weren't far behind.

Other staff members trickled into the station. First, secretary-receptionist-bookkeeper Phyllis Harris arrived to open the office and make the second pot of coffee. Then young Nellie Ward arrived to prepare for her on-air shift, which came right after mine.

Soon after my July arrival in Kotzebue, I was surprised to find in my mailbox a letter from RCA Alascom CEO Stephen Heller. It was a response to the post-resignation letter I had sent him.

In his letter Mr. Heller acknowledged the problems I had described, but he said that the Bethel sales tax problem was beyond RCA's "purview." And that his staff had found no "specific examples" of villages not receiving the billing credits they deserved. That was a little hard to swallow. But Mr. Heller said he knew that RCA had fallen behind their original installation schedule and missed completion target dates. He claimed that the delays were the result of slow approvals from government agencies.[1]

In other words, the delays were someone else's fault. It still sounded like CYA to me.

Responding to my comments about RCA's image in the villages, Mr. Heller said that field crews had been instructed to provide as much "on the spot public relations" as necessary to help villagers to make their telephones "a constructive force in the community."[2]

I wondered if my old field installation crew knew about this.

Mr. Heller concluded his letter by thanking me for my "interest."[3]

The letter did contain a little encouragement. It sounded like the CEO — or at least his staff — had read my letter. Maybe they were paying attention.

But I wasn't satisfied with Mr. Heller's explanation of the credit-for-outages problem. I pushed back in a late August letter, where I said:

> Your explanation of the billing situation is similar to the one I had previously received from RCA and, unless something has changed in the past two months, is not quite correct. Villages report their outages to RCA's Bethel office, and this results in the repair being done, but it does not result in a credit on the village's bill. This is the problem to which I referred in my letter to you and one that I have raised with RCA several times previously.[4]

By that time RCA did have a few more villages' phones working, and I closed my letter with:

> I understand that the telephones in Wales, Diomede, and the villages in the King Salmon - Lake Iliamna area have been turned up. Congratulations on those achievements. I know that the telephones are well appreciated in those villages.[5]

Then, in early October, a little more than a month later, I received another letter from Mr. Heller. It sounded like I might be having at least a small impact.

Heller said that his staff had reviewed the problem of adjusting customer accounts due to outages and that in the future outages would be reported by field offices to headquarters and adjustments would be made to subscribers' bills.[6]

It seemed like a success — but only a small one.

9

KOTZEBUE

NOVEMBER 1973

Nellie Ward sat in the KOTZ lobby, shuffling papers and preparing for her announcer shift. Separated from Nellie by one of the station's big windows, I was still working on air in the control room. I dialed the phone and pushed a button to make a connection to the Kotzebue airport.

Listeners heard:

> This is Don Koutchak at the National Weather Service office in Kotzebue. The forecast for the Kotzebue vicinity and the lower Noatak and Kobuk valleys calls for increasing winds over the next 24 hours as a strong storm system moves north into our area. Southeast winds will reach 30 miles per hour with gusts to 50.

Don continued with a synopsis of the weather map in northwest Alaska, detailed weather forecasts for each of the regions in our listening area, and an aviation report for local pilots. He also gave ice conditions for the Chukchi Sea and Kotzebue Sound. But the big news was the approaching storm. Don didn't need to say that conditions would be dangerous over the next few days. Listeners understood.

Weather forecasts were a critical part of our service. A few times each day we relayed detailed forecasts from Don and his colleagues at their small airport office. The people of the region listened intently, especially when they were planning to travel.

Travel was a big challenge in the Arctic. People moved from village to village by snow machine in winter and small boat in summer, through the vast, windswept landscape, roadless everywhere and treeless near the coast. Bush planes were equipped with emergency supplies — food, sleeping bags and other survival gear. Poor visibility caused by fog, snow, and high winds could force a pilot to make an unexpected landing almost anywhere.

And people traveling by snow machine from village to village needed to know about approaching storms. High winds and blowing snow could hide trails and make travel treacherous. Some trails crossed sea ice, adding another element of danger. Ironically, travel could be most dangerous when the weather was warm. High temperatures signaled storms approaching from the south, bringing high winds and blowing snow, sometimes causing the sea ice to break up. KOTZ weather reports told travelers what to expect.

But before the National Weather Service brought more modern technology to Kotzebue, Ed Ward came up with a way to improve weather forecasts. Ed had lived in Kotzebue for many years, working as a Federal Aviation Administration flight service specialist, a weather forecaster, and — most important to me — a radio telegraph operator and radio ham. His call sign was KL7BVX. Ed could send and receive Morse code at speeds up to 40 words per minute. Local bush pilots depended on Ed for up-to-date weather information and often stopped at his house for a cup of coffee and the latest report on conditions.[1]

9-1 Kotzebue's winters brought heavy snowfall, making it difficult to dig a path into a small house.

Ed knew that northwest Alaska weather systems usually moved from west to east, from eastern Russia to western Alaska. To improve the accuracy of his forecasts, Ed worked out a plan to pick up shortwave weather transmissions from our not-so-friendly neighbor to the west.[2]

First, Ed set out to learn the Russian language. Using a Russian dictionary and a set of Russian language phonograph records, he studied and taught himself to read, write and speak Russian. He had a Russian typewriter with Cyrillic characters. Ed's daughter Nellie told me that, when she was a child, her dad taught her to speak a little Russian. She was overjoyed to discover that the Russian word for her less-than-beloved older brother was "brat."[3]

English: brother

Russian (Cyrillic characters):

Russian (Roman characters): brat

Then Ed expanded his already formidable Morse code skills, mastering all the letters of the Russian alphabet. Many are the same as English letters with the same pattern of dits and dahs, but Russian has letters not used in English, and they have unfamiliar dit-dah patterns. With these extra letters, Ed was ready to listen to weather station transmissions from eastern Russia.[4]

In the attic of his house Ed had racks of radio equipment, including shortwave receivers that could pick up the Russian Morse code transmissions. The Russian stations' shortwave transmissions were loud and clear, easily readable by the experienced Morse operator. Ed Ward had the best weather forecasts around.[5]

In April 1968, about five years before I set foot in Kotzebue, Ed became a hero when he helped save the lives of a Kotzebue pilot and a group of polar bear hunters, some of the many hunters who flocked to Kotzebue for the spring polar bear hunt held in those days. The group had crash landed, and they were stranded on the ice of the Chukchi Sea somewhere to the northwest of Kotzebue.[6]

The hunters had not filed a flight plan, but, when they were reported missing, Ed began a radio search. He suspected that their flight path was the same one taken by other polar bear hunters. After hours of transmitting, Ed's receiver crackled, and he heard a faint signal. He thought that the radio transmitter aboard the downed aircraft might have been damaged in the crash but that the plane's receiver might still be working.[7]

Ed transmitted again, asking the hunters to wiggle their radio's battery lead if they could hear his transmission. They responded. Ed worked out a yes or no sequence, asking them to do one thing for "yes" and a different thing for "no."[8]

9-2 Ed Ward received a FAA award for helping to save the polar bear hunters.

The hunters didn't know Morse code, but Ed used voice transmissions to ask them questions. Slowly, through a series of questions and answers, Ed deduced the likely location of the aircraft. Search and rescue aircraft were dispatched from Kotzebue. When the search aircraft were close to the hunters' position, Ed again communicated with the downed aircraft, using the yes-no system to pinpoint their location. The pilot and hunters were picked up and returned safely to Kotzebue.[9]

After I'd been on the job for a few months, Marv asked me to travel to Anchorage to talk to the commissioners of the AEBC. They wanted a report on KOTZ, Alaska's newest public radio station. And that's when I first met Augie Hiebert in person. He was one of the commissioners.

I climbed aboard an Alaska Airlines jet to fly to Anchorage, and at the meeting the next day, I told the commissioners about our station's revised program schedule, its technical operation, and its finances. Augie and the other commissioners seemed happy with my report.

Then there was a break, and I talked with Augie. I already knew about his work building KFAR, the first radio station in Fairbanks. We had common interests in ham radio, experiences building radio systems in Alaska and a mutual desire to serve the Alaska public.

There were similarities between KFAR in 1939 and KOTZ in 1973. Both stations provided vital services and popular entertainment to their listeners. The message services allowing listeners to submit messages to be read on the air were the same at both stations. At KFAR the service was called "Tundra Topics." At KOTZ it was "Tundra Telegraph." KFAR sent out major-league baseball games. KOTZ had "Old Time Radio" and

"Eskimo Stories." In 1939 KFAR had been the talk of Fairbanks. In 1973 KOTZ was the talk of Kotzebue.

Showing no concern about competition to his commercial stations, Augie was an avid supporter of public broadcasting. He became a member of the AEBC, and he was enthusiastic about the commission's work bringing radio broadcasting to rural Alaska.[10]

Augie and I talked again during a second break in the meeting. He wanted to hear about my problems working with the bush telephone program. I was surprised to hear that Augie had ideas similar to mine about using satellite communication systems to provide telephone — and even television — services to Alaska villages. Augie told me that he had been thinking about the satellite technology's potential in Alaska for many years. We agreed to stay in touch.

The next day I was aboard an Alaska Airlines jet headed back to Kotzebue.

Soon after my return to Kotzebue I received a call from Lee Wareham, then RCA's outlying area supervisor for the Fairbanks district. Lee and his partner Cliff Scheel were traveling around Alaska aboard a post-World War II C-82 "flying boxcar," which also carried a transportable satellite earth station. Lee and Cliff were checking the feasibility of using satellite communications in the Alaska bush, testing reception of satellite signals from a Canadian satellite and checking the quality of television broadcasts from the satellite.[11]

I answered the phone and heard Lee ask: "Do you have space for us to stay at your place?"[12]

He and Cliff needed a place to stay for the few days they would need to be in Kotzebue to set up the earth station, make signal strength measurements, dismantle the station and fly on to their next test location.[13]

I quickly said, "Sure. The cabin's pretty small but it's warm and there's room to sleep on the floor. Make sure you have sleeping bags."[14]

A few days later the C-82 landed in Kotzebue. Lee and Cliff soon showed up at my cabin, where I had food and drinks ready. Three tech guys stayed up late that night swapping stories. We all had stories to tell, and some of them may have been true.[15]

My little cabin was only 24 by 36 feet. Its "pot burner" stove kept us warm that night. The little stove used number two heating oil and always worked, even during power outages. As I drifted off to sleep, I heard the stove's weighted damper valve banging against its housing as wind gusts blew across the cabin's roof. It lulled me to sleep, but Lee later told me that the damper's unfamiliar sound made it hard for him to sleep, waking him up throughout the night. But Cliff slept well and voiced no complaints.[16]

The satellite earth station Lee and Cliff were carrying used a 16-foot antenna, qualifying it as a small earth station, the kind of station that might be feasible for use in Alaska's rural villages. As part of the bubbling controversy about using small satellite earth stations in Alaska villages, RCA had asked Lee and Cliff to find out whether the Canadian Anik satellite had enough spillover signal to reach beyond Canada and into western and northern Alaska. This was important, because, at the time, there were no other satellites in orbit that RCA deemed suitable for service to Alaska villages.[17]

RCA's signal measurement mission started at Adak in the Aleutian Islands and moved from there to King Salmon and Bethel in southwest Alaska. In Bethel Lee and Cliff took over from the project's first measurement team. When the measurements in Bethel were complete, Lee and Cliff had moved north to Nome and then came to Kotzebue. After spending a few nights at my cabin, they flew on to Barrow, Deadhorse, and Fort Yukon to complete the measurements.[18]

The RCA team's measurement project had resulted, in a way, from Augie Hiebert's efforts. In 1971 Augie visited COMSAT headquarters in Washington DC, where he saw a small satellite earth station, one with a 4.5 meter (16 foot) diameter antenna. Augie wondered if antennas like this one would work at Alaska's northern latitudes.[19]

After some investigation Augie became an advocate for the use of satellite communication in Alaska villages. He thought that small satellite earth stations, far smaller than the 98-foot Bartlett earth station, could be used throughout Alaska. And he thought that the small stations could be built and operated at low cost, providing a practical solution for the villages.[20]

But RCA disagreed. The company conceded that earth stations could be used in rural Alaska, but they said the earth stations could be no smaller than 10 meters and that these larger stations should be installed only in large towns — regional centers like Nome, Kotzebue, Barrow, Bethel, and Dillingham. There was disagreement even among engineers about whether small earth stations would work at all.[21]

To help to settle the question, Augie wanted COMSAT to demonstrate the use of a 4.5 meter earth station in Alaska to determine whether small earth stations would work in the north. Augie became chairman of Gov. Egan's Telecommunications Advisory Committee, which coordinated the demonstration project for the state of Alaska. But RCA opposed the project.[22]

Building on the success of COMSAT's Bartlett earth station in Talkeetna, Augie drafted a letter for Gov. Egan's signature, requesting that COMSAT carry out a television demonstration in rural Alaska. The letter explained:

> The project's goal... is to prove that high-quality television and voice transmission can be achieved through the use of satellites and small, low-cost earth stations. This must be achieved if Alaska's far-flung and remote communities are to enjoy the many kinds of information which Americans in other states have long taken for granted.[23]

The letter that Augie drafted for Gov. Egan resulted in COMSAT's agreement to demonstrate the use of small earth stations for video and audio communication in several locations around the state. COMSAT's announcement said that the project would:

> demonstrate the advantage of satellite communications in meeting the unique communications requirements of small communities in remote areas, to determine the effects of extreme climatic conditions on satellite communications and analyze possible interference from the aurora borealis.[24]

COMSAT's demonstration project was done in May and June 1972. Their first satellite test was done in Alaska's capital city of Juneau, which, like Anchorage and Fairbanks, received national television programs only by videotapes that were mailed to its local stations — not exactly instant communication.

That might have been OK for "All in the Family," "The Mary Tyler Moore Show," "Maude," and other sitcoms of the day. But the locals were hungry for live broadcasts of the news and — probably more urgently — baseball, football and basketball games. There were even a few unconfirmed stories circulating about innocent sports fans placing bets on games that had been played days earlier.

Juneau's news junkies and sports fans were getting tired of those delayed broadcasts, and that's why the COMSAT demonstration captured their imaginations.

On May 4, 1972, the *Southeast Alaska Empire* reported about the COMSAT project:

> A television signal traveling 45,000 miles at the speed of light brought Juneau its first taste of space-age communications last night. An hour's television broadcast from Anchorage to Juneau via satellite went off without a hitch. It was the opening segment of the demonstration designed to show that existing satellite technology can overcome the communications problems posed by Alaska's vast and rugged expanses.[25]

Using the INTELSAT IV satellite positioned over the Pacific Ocean, the small, transportable COMSAT earth station moved on from Juneau to demonstrate its capabilities in Kodiak, Bethel, Nome, Barrow, and Fort Yukon, spending three days at each location. In between the demonstrations, the earth station was disassembled, transported by Alaska's Air National Guard, and reassembled at its next location. Television transmissions were successfully received at all the locations, and the project was declared a success.[26]

In its report to the FCC, COMSAT said:

> The recently completed Alaskan program served two major purposes. First it successfully demonstrated the capability of a small aperture earth station for receiving television and providing voice communications in remote areas. Second, tests and investigations were conducted which provided information for assessing the operation of earth stations under conditions found at high northern latitudes.[27]

9-3 Nome was among the towns where COMSAT demonstrated the operation of a small satellite earth station.

COMSAT had clearly demonstrated the feasibility of small earth stations in Alaska. They would work even in the far north. But the successful COMSAT demonstration project seemed to have caused concern at RCA headquarters. The company may have worried that COMSAT wanted to provide telecommunication services in Alaska, a big threat to RCA's dominant position in the state.

RCA's 1973 tests of the coverage of the Canadian Anik satellite may have been a response to this threat. If COMSAT could serve Alaska by using INTELSAT IV, RCA could do the same using Anik, and that was shown by RCA's 1973 tests, which reached pretty much the same conclusion as the COMSAT demonstration.

With two successful tests of small satellite earth stations in rural Alaska- — one by COMSAT and one by RCA — I was optimistic we would soon have a better communication system for Alaska villages. The deployment of small satellite earth stations, which could be used for television, telephone and other kinds of communication, seemed two steps closer.

Still, I wondered if the successful tests had really convinced RCA's executives that satellite communication was the right technology for Alaska's villages.

I thought my new pen pal, the RCA Alaska CEO, might tell me.

10

KOTZEBUE

DECEMBER 1973

When I began the broadcast day as "Alex in the Morning," people for miles around were listening. Sometimes I called myself *Umik*, Inupiaq for "beard" or "whiskers." Like some of the other local characters, I sported the facial foliage that justified the name. Listeners were amused.

It seemed that everyone in northwest Alaska knew me. It was the power of radio.

I hoped people would tune in at the very beginning of our broadcast day, and I started the Early Bird Club, whose membership was open to all who could name the first song of the day. There was no tangible benefit to being a member of the club, but I said there was "prestige." I regularly read the names of new members, and listeners across northwest Alaska knew who was on the Early Bird Club roster.

The first song each morning might have been Lynn Anderson singing "I Never Promised You a Rose Garden" or "Joy to the World" by The Three Dog Night, but one listener wrote in and said the first song of the day had been the "Alaska Flag Song," part of our morning sign-on tape. I couldn't argue with that one. I made the listener a member but also changed the rules a bit to close that little loophole.

In another morning feature, I invited schoolteachers from across our large listening area to send their students' songs, stories and poems on cassette tapes, to be broadcast as part of the morning show. Soon our receptionist and bookkeeper Phyllis Harris was unwrapping myriad small packages containing tapes arriving in the mail.

10-1 "Alex in the Morning" broadcasting from the KOTZ studio.

Schoolteachers — and parents — from across our large listening area were eager to share the kids' talents, and hearing the tapes on the air made them proud. Like other radio features, this one helped to temper the isolation of living in an Alaskan village. The cassette tapes, Tundra Telegrams, song dedications, Eskimo stories, and local newscasts interconnected the people of northwest Alaska.

After my early morning on-air shift, I listened to KOTZ on the speaker in my office.

Our air signal carried the voices of young announcers Joe Hill, Carolyn Smith, Nellie and her brother Delbert. All recent graduates of Kotzebue's high school, the four announcers spread their youthful energy to the distant villages. Their voices conveyed pride in the new station and the service they were providing.

Carolyn had an important announcement for one of the villages:

"Health aide Lucy up in Kiana has flu shots available for all the kids, but *umuk* the babies (carry them on your back inside a warm parka) because it's cold out there!"

Nellie happily read an invitation to a listener's friends and neighbors in another village:

"My cousin in Noorvik wants to let all the village people know that she made lots of *akutaq*, and she wants to share it tonight. Come on over if you want some." ("Eskimo ice cream," you may recall, is made from blueberries in whipped reindeer tallow, seal oil and water.)

At the age of 18 Nellie was a memorable character. She was full of life. Her broad cheeks and straight, black hair betrayed her mother's ancestry. With an Inupiaq mother and a white father, Nellie had learned to live in two worlds. Equally at ease wearing a *kuspuk*[1] and eating *akutaq* at a village celebration, or interviewing visiting state officials about government policy, she was irreverent in a way that made me laugh.

"That guy from Anchorage was really full of …" she said.

Nellie's charm and dry humor flowed through the microphone and spread across northwest Alaska. She was a star.[2]

Joe Hill had spirit, too. A year younger than Nellie, Joe was of medium height and powerfully built. He was interested in radio technology, and he sometimes helped me as I did my engineering

10-2 Unafraid of VIPs, Nellie interviewed Gov. Jay Hammond
when he visited Kotzebue

tasks, eager to pitch in and asking lots of questions. Joe lived with
his mother and stepfather, who managed a general store in town.
He had graduated from high school just a few months before my
arrival in Kotzebue and, like Nellie, had a sharp, dry sense of
humor. We traded good-natured jabs.

"Is that really how you do things back in the big city?" he asked
with a smirk.

Carolyn and Delbert were good announcers and faithful employees, but they didn't push back like Nellie and Joe. They brought

steadiness to the station. So did secretary-receptionist Phyllis, who was older than the rest of us. She was our den mother.

The heart of KOTZ's programming was the music — a blend of Top 40 and country and western. Among our top tunes in 1973, our first year on the air, were:

"Top of the World" — The Carpenters

"Bad, Bad Leroy Brown" — Jim Croce

"Delta Dawn" — Helen Reddy

"Killing Me Softly with His Song" — Roberta Flack

"Tie a Yellow Ribbon Round the Old Oak Tree" — Tony Orlando and Dawn

"You're So Vain" — Carly Simon

"Kodachrome" — Paul Simon

"Satin Sheets" — Jeanne Pruett

"Why Me?" — Kris Kristofferson

As I listened, pen in hand, to the music on my office's "air monitor" speaker, I drafted a letter to Alascom CEO Stephen Heller. I knew that RCA was planning to put some large satellite earth stations in some of Alaska's regional centers but no small earth stations in the villages. I focused on the village situation in my letter. I began:

> Dear Mr. Heller:
>
> I was pleased to learn that RCA recently received the required approvals to go ahead with a satellite communication system. The advent of communications by satellite could have a dramatic impact on Alaska's remote villages.[3]

After a few paragraphs emphasizing the importance of a modern communication system to Alaska's villagers, I continued by saying:

> The alternative to a land-based relay system is, of course, a satellite system with ground stations in the villages. Such a system, I think, would be capable of providing reliable service. Although the cost of a satellite ground station is high, it would seem that, if the RCA Corporation brought its resources to bear on the problem, the costs could be reduced to make such a system economically feasible. We hear much these days about low-cost ground stations. I would think that, if anyone can do it, RCA can.
>
> Mr. Heller, it is impossible for me to overstate the seriousness of the rural communications problem. Its impact on the village people is tremendous. I feel that RCA should waste no time in providing a reliable communication system. Isn't that a satellite system?[4]

About two weeks later I received his response. Using a friendly tone, Mr. Heller told me that RCA was considering using satellite communications in rural Alaska but that they were concerned about "incurring enormous costs." He said they were evaluating the "cost factors" in order to be alert to the "proper time to change our plans."[5]

The letter was cordial, but Stephen Heller still seemed unconvinced about the virtues of using satellite communications to serve the villages.

11

KOTZEBUE

DECEMBER 1973

Northwest Alaska's villages buzzed with the news of KOTZ's arrival. One of the villages was Kivalina, perched on a gravel barrier island along the coast of the Chukchi Sea 85 miles above the Arctic Circle. For centuries the people of Kivalina had subsisted on the animals they took from land and sea. Small, wood frame houses dotting the gravel spit had replaced the traditional sod huts that once provided shelter.

Kivalina's people combined their traditional subsistence lifestyle with modern technology and a cash-based economy. The men of the village used long nets to fish for salmon, and they used rifles to hunt whale, walrus and seal. On land they hunted for caribou, often using snow machines instead of more traditional dog teams. The women of the village cut the harvested fish and meat, and, following tradition, hung it on outdoor racks to dry.

The women also sewed, making clothing for their families. They used animal skins from the men's hunting expeditions and modern fabrics they found in catalogs, ordering by mail from "Outside," as Alaskans called anywhere outside the state.

Some of the villagers worked for paychecks at the village school or store. These jobs, along with welfare checks received from the state, gave the villagers some cash, allowing them to order rifles, snow machines, fabrics, and other products from Outside.

11-1 Kivalina sits on a gravel barrier island 85 miles above the Arctic Circle.

At times all of Kivalina's villagers gathered in the community hall, the biggest building in the village, to dance to the beat of traditional drums. The men of the village used wooden sticks to hit dried seal skin stretched across big wooden hoops while other men bobbed up and down, dancing and rhythmically reenacting activities like hunting for seals. Later *kuspuk*-clad women dancers took over, visually telling their own stories.

Kivalina's cultural activities were important. Dancing, traditional foods, and *potlatches*, known to non-Natives as "potlucks," were at the core of village life throughout northwest Alaska.

News of the new radio station spread across the region, and people adapted their daily routines to include time for listening to

KOTZ. With its mix of local news, country and Top 40 music, weather, information, and news from Outside, KOTZ was popular. Some folks listened throughout the day from sign-on to sign-off.

KOTZ had made the radio a focus of each family's home. We poured music, news, and information from across the region into their houses, and we connected them to friends and relatives in other villages. At night, as the wind outside roared, sweeping snow across the gravel barrier island, folks huddled close to the radio, intent on the stories we aired.

On our "Eskimo Stories" program, the region's elders took turns telling traditional stories in the Inupiaq language. Some of them were old enough to remember the introduction of reindeer to western Alaska in the early twentieth century. Through their stories, the elders helped to preserve the vanishing oral legends of the Inupiaq of northwest Alaska. After they passed on, other elders followed, and the program continues today, renamed "Inupiaq Stories."

My favorite storyteller was Kotzebue's Mamie Beaver. Sometimes I visited Mamie in her compact house near the beach and overlooking Kotzebue Sound. It wasn't far from my own cabin.

I knocked on the weather-beaten door and heard Mamie's tiny voice say "Come in, *Umik*." She liked to remind me that she had originally given me the Inupiaq name.

Mamie was always sitting on the tiny bed squeezed into her little house. She was petite, and her advanced age made her a bit frail. I often found her sewing together animal skins, creating an item of clothing.

Mamie always commented about something I had said on the radio that day, usually gently teasing me because I had misunderstood or misstated some aspect of local geography or culture. It seemed that Mamie listened to KOTZ all day every day, never missing anything that was said on the radio. She was a treasure, and I was glad to have her as a friend and a storyteller on "Eskimo Stories."

At night we also had "Old Time Radio," but, in northwest Alaska, the programs weren't really old. An enterprising company was syndicating radio shows of the 1930s, 1940s and 1950s, sending them to radio stations across the United States on tape. Every few weeks we received a box of 30-minute tapes with programs like "The Lone Ranger," "The Shadow," and "The Green Hornet."

In early evening, listeners heard the "William Tell Overture," the opening theme for the Lone Ranger — or the Shadow's opening line, "Who knows what evil lurks in the hearts of men?" A 30-minute drama from the past followed. It was intended to be radio nostalgia. But for most KOTZ listeners, it was a new kind of entertainment. Most of our listeners had never before heard these radio dramas. People loved them!

After KOTZ had been on the air for about a year, Ruthie Ramoth joined us as an announcer. Ruthie had a unique skill. Born and raised in the nearby village of Selawik, she was fluent in both English and Inupiaq. On the air she interweaved the two languages in a way that allowed all listeners to understand perfectly by listening to either the English or Inupiaq words.

First Ruthie spoke a little English, then a little Inupiaq, then back to English, and back and forth again. She was fluent in both languages, and she effortlessly glided from one to the other with no loss of rhythm or meaning. She was young, but she felt a sense of mission to help to preserve her native language. Ruthie later joined the University of Alaska, contributing to projects aimed at preserving the Inupiaq language and culture.

We worked hard to connect the villages, and listeners expressed their appreciation. Each day fan mail arrived at the station, carrying gratitude for the work we were doing at KOTZ. Many contained song requests, which we did our best to fulfill, and some contained drawings of "Alex in the Morning." At first the drawings were unsolicited, but, after a while, we decided to give a prize for the best drawing, to be chosen, of course, by a panel of impartial judges. For weeks drawings arrived at the station. We posted them on walls until all vertical surfaces were covered. In the end the winner was judged to be none other than Mamie Beaver, who had created a life-size painting of yours truly, complete with wolverine fur for the beard. It was Mamie's way of reminding me that she was the one who first called me *Umik*.

And our mailbox was full of song requests and dedications. They might have seemed corny to a city listener, but they were important to our listeners. The requests were usually for country tunes and accompanied by personal messages going from a listener in one village to a friend, family member, or lover in another village.

Carolyn announced:

"This next tune is going out to Susie in Kiana from Chester in Noorvik. 'I miss you Susie. I'm coming up to Kiana to see you over the weekend. Love, Chester.'"

Then we played Chester's request, Tammy Wynette singing "Stand By Your Man."

> *Stand by your man*
> *Give him two arms to cling to*
> *And something warm to come to*
> *when nights are cold and lonely*

Stand by your man

And tell the world you love him

Keep giving all the love you can

Stand by your man

Stand by your man

And show the world you love him

Keep giving all the love you can

Stand by your man

But some dedications were not so loving.

Carolyn again:

"This next tune is going out to Molly in Shungnak from Eddie in Ambler. Eddie says 'My message to you is in the words of this tune.' Here's Carly Simon, singing 'You're So Vain!'"

You're so vain

You probably think this song is about you

You're so vain, you're so vain

I'll bet you think this song is about you

Don't you?

Don't you?

The telephone never stopped ringing at KOTZ. Listeners called to send the messages we called "Tundra Telegrams," personal messages directed to family and friends in other villages.

Delbert intoned:

"Uncle Willie, my plane arrives in your village at 6:30. Please meet me at the runway."

And another message from Delbert:

"Sister Rachel, Granny left her medicine on the dresser. Send it as soon as possible."

Tundra Telegrams informed extended families in the outlying villages of the passing of a loved one. Or they told the happy news of the birth of a new family member. In harsh weather the messages were a rallying call for volunteers to search for a missing snowmobiler or dog musher. If a family home was destroyed by fire, they called for donations. The message service was essential. With no phones in the villages, KOTZ was often the only available means of communication.

Other radio stations across rural Alaska sent similar messages. Each station had its own name for the service — our Tundra Telegrams were Village Hotlines or Caribou Clatters elsewhere. It was technically illegal for a broadcast station to send a personal message, but the FCC recognized the importance of the services and focused its attention elsewhere.

Services like "Tundra Telegrams" highlighted the inadequate communication systems in villages across Alaska.

12

KOTZEBUE

MAY 1974

Far to our south and east, a few Alaska villages were beginning to experience the pleasures of commercial broadcast television. The Alaska Educational Broadcasting Commission — the AEBC — had tried an experiment by installing low-power "mini-TV" transmitters and video cassette players in a few villages. Broadcasts were recorded back in the cities by tuning in their television stations. Then the tapes were sent out to the villages.

Using the terminology of the day, the tapes were said to be "bicycled" to the villages, but they actually traveled via U.S. mail aboard airplanes, first to one village and then to another. The FCC granted special waivers of their regulations to make the mini-TV transmitters legal, and the villagers bought television sets. They were watching weeks-old programs, but they were happy!

The first two mini-TV stations were installed in 1971 and 1972, before Marv Weatherly's arrival at the AEBC. These first stations were installed in the interior village of Fort Yukon and the southeast Alaska village of Angoon. Later, in 1973, as AEBC's engineer, Marv installed more mini-TV stations at St. Paul,

Unalaska, and Whittier. The "lash up" was a little crude, but it hinted of things to come.[1]

I knew that Alaska's villages couldn't receive same-day television shows without satellite communications, and, of course, most villages still had no phone service. The villages really needed satellite earth stations. Marv and Augie were both working on it. They kept me informed about their push toward a satellite communication network for the villages, and I tried to add a small bit of support with my letters to Mr. Heller.

In May 1974 I sent him one that said:

> The people of our area have heard much recently about the advances being made by RCA in improving the state's communication system. We have noted particularly the rapid work being done by RCA on communication facilities to serve the trans-Alaska pipeline. We have even been told that Robert Sarnoff will be given an honorary degree by the University of Alaska.[2] Yet, with all this news, the villages of northwest Alaska appear to have no immediate prospects for improved communications.
>
> During the past year we have learned that low-cost satellite ground stations that could be installed in villages are both technologically and economically feasible.
>
> We were happy to hear a few months ago that RCA was joining with representatives of the governor's office, Stanford University, and the Air Force to study the implementation of the village satellite communication system. But now the construction season is almost here and we have heard of no plans to build such a system.

The fact of poor communications is an obvious hardship, but it becomes far less digestible when one is aware of the alternatives. Surely RCA must now recognize its responsibility as Alaska's long-distance carrier and provide service to the rural areas with the same fast action it exhibits in more profitable places.[3]

Mr. Heller's response was disappointing. He talked about the pending installation of midsize 10-meter earth stations in Nome and Bethel, but there wasn't much in his letter about the small earth stations that were needed in Alaska's villages. He said that RCA continued to study the "smaller stations as a logical, cost-effective alternate to the terrestrial bush telephone program we have been pursuing" and that details of such a plan would be released later.[4]

It was pretty clear that Mr. Heller and others at RCA still weren't convinced.

A year earlier I had met a pretty young nurse in Nome, and I had soon invited Meg Gabriel to move to Kotzebue, telling her it was a nice, friendly town. She liked the idea, and when a nursing job opened at the Kotzebue hospital, she applied. Meg was soon hired and moved north.

Kotzebue's hospital nurses had living accommodations that were luxurious by local standards. The hospital was part of the U.S. government's Indian Health Service, and its professional staff lived in government-owned buildings.

In her comfortable apartment, Meg was sheltered from the day-to-day realities of most Kotzebue residents — tending a cabin's heating stove, checking for frozen pipes, and hauling water, if

12-1 Meg liked living in Kotzebue.

needed. For most people, life in the Arctic winter had some challenges, but for Meg and her colleagues, the heat always worked, the electricity was always on, and life was good. I didn't mind visiting Meg when my electricity was off — or any other time I wanted to sample a bit of the good life.

By September 1974 Meg and I were working on wedding plans. We had postponed the planning until the end of commercial fishing season because, well, we were busy fishing. The result was a November wedding with weather far from that preferred by June brides in the smaller states. Nellie handled the logistics.

We were married in the Kotzebue teen center, a long, narrow wood frame building, usually used for dances and other teenage social events. But, on a cold and windy Saturday afternoon in November, it was the site of our wedding ceremony.

12-2 Meg sometimes rode on the runners of the sled I pulled with my snow machine.

Meg was radiant in her white wedding gown, and I was decked out in a blue sport jacket that she had made me. Our wedding rings were made of ivory carved from walrus tusks. The vows were led by magistrate Ross Schaeffer, and Rick Draper, the local Episcopal priest, did some religious readings.

The teen center was packed. The ceremony was followed by a reception, complete with a dance performance by the Inupiaq elders of Kotzebue. The drummers' sticks tapped on wooden hoops and against seal skin stretched across the hoops. The drummers chanted, and the dancers bobbed first left and then right.

Lucy Jensen was the leader of the dancers. Totally blind, she wore dark glasses, but she was a commanding presence as she led the dancers. The Inupiaq dancers were in rare form, drumming and dancing with energy. We were honored by their presence.

Soon everyone, Inupiaq and white, young and old, was dancing — even our parents, who had traveled 4000 miles from the East Coast. The expressions on their faces revealed, though, that their life in the East had left them unprepared for such an experience.

13

KOTZEBUE

AUGUST 1974

I followed the news from my Arctic vantage point.

Alaska was scheduled to elect a new governor in November 1974, and the primary election would be held in August. Gov. Bill Egan was running for reelection. There were two Republican challengers, Walter Hickel, a former governor, and Bristol Bay Borough mayor Jay Hammond. It seemed likely that the well-known Hickel would defeat Hammond and face Egan in the November general election.

The two leading candidates found a campaign issue in the villages' communication problems, and it looked to them like a satellite system was the answer. Candidate Hickel learned that the RCA corporation was planning to launch a new satellite and that the satellite would be positioned to cover Alaska. But RCA had no plans to use it to serve Alaska's villages.

Hickel saw an opportunity to attack Alaska's sitting governor, and he wrote a letter to the Federal Communications Commission — the FCC — saying, "Our governor should be demanding this satellite serve all villages of a certain size. Instead he is letting it drift, which could cost our Native people up-to-date communications for more than a decade."[1]

But Gov. Egan had already been working on the problem with his advisers, including Marv, who was by then AEBC executive director. Egan gave the press the letters he had previously written to the FCC and RCA. The campaign squabble drew public attention to the challenges of providing communication service to the villages.

The issue had already become known throughout Alaska's officialdom if not to the public. The Canadians had launched their Anik satellite to provide communication service to small Canadian villages in the north. COMSAT had demonstrated the appeal of satellites to serve rural Alaska. The ATS-1 satellite project had provided reliable communication services to 26 sites, most of them villages, across rural Alaska.[2] [3]

There was also interest in Washington D.C. The U.S. Department of Health Education and Welfare had seen through the ATS-1 project how satellites could help the delivery of health services to rural Alaskans. And Alaska's U.S. Senator Ted Stevens was getting interested.

Insiders were aware of the interplay among RCA and state and federal agencies. They were starting to understand that satellite communication technology provided a technologically and economically effective way to provide reliable communication services to Alaska's villages.[4]

Even though Walter Hickel raised the village telecommunication issue as part of his campaign to be governor, in the end it didn't help him. Hickel was upset in the August primary election by Jay Hammond, a guide, bush pilot, and former legislator well known in the Bristol Bay area of Alaska but without Hickel's statewide name recognition. Still, Hammond won the primary.[5]

And after he upset Hickel, Jay Hammond pulled off a surprise victory in November, defeating incumbent Gov. Bill Egan in the general election. Hammond was inaugurated governor a month later.

That was when Marv Weatherly saw an opening.

Soon after his December inauguration, Gov. Jay Hammond appointed Marv to be director of the Office of Telecommunications, a small unit within the governor's office. The office had only one responsibility, to advise the governor on telecommunications matters. Jay came from rural Alaska, and he knew that communication service was a big deal out there. With Marv's help, the new governor quickly set up a telecommunications working group, which included telecommunications experts and other interested parties.[6]

13-1 Marv Weatherly became Gov. Hammond's telecommunications director.

The telecommunications working group and the state's consultants saw that RCA's bush telephone program was foundering. Marv and other members of the governor's team agreed that the use of small satellite stations in Alaska's villages could provide far better service to the villages than RCA's VHF radio phone program, and they wanted RCA to use small earth stations to provide telecommunication services to the villages.[7]

One of the state's consultants, Bob Walp, later recalled:

> We may have lacked experience, but our plan proved to be sound. We argued over the practicality of putting small stations in the villages and even the feasibility of ever using small earth stations. Costs, timing and schedules were discussed. RCA's approach was based upon equipment that was in use at that time; this was conservative and relatively risk free. But it was based upon practices used for trunking heavy traffic between international centers, not for thin line circuits to tiny towns, and used the satellite inefficiently. We had spent a lot of time analyzing the small station in each village and knew that it was economically feasible.[8]

The battle lines were quickly drawn. Things came to a head in January 1975 when Marv led a public meeting to review RCA's plans. On one side of the table were Marv and his team, representing the state of Alaska. Across the table were RCA Alascom president Stephen Heller, once my pen pal, and representatives from RCA's corporate offices in New Jersey.[9]

After the meeting, Mr. Heller invited Marv and consultant Bob Walp to lunch at the Petroleum Club in downtown Anchorage. It turned out to be an emotional lunch.

Heller adamantly refused to pursue the small earth station option.

Marv said: "Dammit, Steve, if RCA doesn't put in small earth stations, the state will!"[10]

Heller replied, "Be my guest!"[11]

That was quite an invitation.

Bob Walp recalled:

> After lunch, Marv and I walked back to his office at 308 G Street, a few blocks away. By the time we got out of the cold we had concluded, "Why not?" [This touched off] a chain of events that eventually put a small earth station in every Alaska village. Marv quickly got in touch with selected members of the state legislature, receiving strong indications of interest and support for state-owned earth stations if that was the way to get communications to rural Alaska. There were well over 100 unserved communities at the time, we estimated. To get things started, we decided to request funds for 100 small earth stations and worry about their location later. Because the legislature is mandated to end its session in the spring, there was no time to analyze needs in a methodical manner.[12] [13]

Marv knew what he needed to do. He quickly set about working with key legislators to get an appropriation of $5 million, which was the amount Marv and the consultants believed would be needed to buy the equipment to build small earth stations for 100 Alaska villages.

Here's how Marv remembered it:

> I needed $5 million. That was the magic figure. I went to [Democratic Senators] Jay Kertulla and Chancy Croft. RCA was all set up to kill this thing

in the Senate — my request for the $5 million. But the House — that was no problem. The Senate was the battleground. Now here we have a Republican governor and Republican cabinet. I was a Republican. My opposition in the Senate was from the Republicans.[14]

Senators Croft and Kerttula were able to get the job done.

Marv continued:

> Jay [Hammond] called me on the phone. He says "are you sitting down?" I said, "Hell, I'm in bed." And he says "You got your $5 million. Now go out and build it." And you could hear my yells from one end of Anchorage to the other. I took the $5 million and started procurement.[15]

But the battle was not yet won. The state and RCA carried the fight to the Federal Communications Commission, where they disagreed over technical and economic issues. There was bitterness on both sides. But with $5 million in his pocket, Marv was holding an "ace" — the state's financial ability to go out, buy the equipment needed for 100 earth stations, and install it in the villages.

It was no surprise that RCA saw a threat to their position as Alaska's only long-distance telephone provider. They wondered if the state of Alaska would really be bold enough to go into business as a competing long-distance telephone provider. Bob Walp remembered Marv's wrangling with RCA as "a high stakes poker game."[16]

Eventually, under the threat of having the state of Alaska as a competitor, RCA agreed to install the 100 small earth stations using equipment purchased and provided by the state. RCA Alascom would operate the stations as part of its own network, but ultimate ownership of the earth stations would be decided at a later time. The agreement was signed by both parties in July 1975.[17]

Marv and his team thought this was just fine. They realized that the state didn't have the expertise to operate a telecommunication network that would provide service to the public. RCA did have that expertise. Marv was satisfied because rural Alaska would soon have a better communication system. RCA was satisfied because they would keep their monopoly as Alaska's only long-distance carrier.

And things were looking up for people living in Alaska's villages.

14

KOTZEBUE

NOVEMBER 1974

Kotzebue was the only community in the region with telephone service, but the phone service wasn't great. In fact, it was terrible!

RCA was Alaska's long-distance telephone company, but our local phone service was provided by North State Telephone, a small company owned by a crusty Arkansas native named John Gilbert. His company had been granted authority by the Alaska Public Utilities Commission — the APUC — to provide telephone service to Kotzebue and three other towns in Alaska. We wondered if their service was as bad as ours.

Our calls were often disconnected for no apparent reason, there were many other service interruptions, and there were plenty of billing problems. Long periods of time passed when neither Gilbert nor anyone else from North State Telephone was even present in Kotzebue to fix the problems.

But rural Alaskans are patient and good-natured. They knew that the APUC was responsible for overseeing telephone service. They knew that the agency was supposed to receive complaints about the service of telephone companies and other utilities. Still,

Kotzebue's people just lived with the problems.

But that began to change in the winter of 1973-74.

Across rural Alaska high school basketball is a big deal. When Kotzebue's high school team, the Huskies, played on their home court, the gym was packed with basketball fans. When the team went on a road trip, all the radios in town were tuned to KOTZ for the live broadcast of every game. People followed the action minute-by-minute.

As the KOTZ engineer, I traveled with the Kotzebue team when they played in other western Alaska towns. The team's "road trips" were made by plane because towns in western Alaska aren't interconnected by roads.

On one road trip, coach Jim Holcomb, sportscaster Brad Wilson, the ballplayers, and I flew aboard a twin-engine Cessna that carried us to Dillingham, a town about the same size as Kotzebue but 550 miles to our south.

Once in Dillingham I scrambled to make the radio hookup. The people of Kotzebue were counting on me to deliver the game's broadcast to them.

The Dillingham gym was about 100 yards from the nearest telephone, and I spent an hour stringing surplus army "battle wire" across a vacant field from the gym to the phone, where I connected the wire. I would use the phone to make a long-distance call to send the game to the KOTZ studio.

With the game about to start, everything was set. Coach Jim Holcomb and the team were on the court. Announcer Brad Wilson was at the mike. Nellie was at the controls in the KOTZ studio. We started to broadcast.

But in the second quarter our over-the-air signal went quiet. Brad Wilson's voice was no longer there to describe the action. Kotzebue's sports fans heard nothing. KOTZ went to "dead air" — silence.

Nellie quickly realized that the telephone connection had been interrupted, and at first she thought there was a technical glitch somewhere between Dillingham and Kotzebue. She dialed the local telephone exchange, where John Gilbert was working. He told her that he had purposely interrupted the broadcast because he had another need for that circuit. The game was important to the people of Kotzebue, but Gilbert didn't care. He refused to reconnect the broadcast, and Kotzebue's listeners missed the rest of the game.

The fans were furious! This was worse than disconnected phone calls, billing problems, and other complaints. This was basketball! The people of Kotzebue wouldn't stand for missing their basketball broadcast. John Gilbert had gone too far.

At the general store and in the post office, people began to talk about all the telephone problems they had experienced with North State Telephone over the years. But interrupting a basketball broadcast? It was the last straw!

Soon the Mauneluk Association,[1] the regional Native nonprofit corporation for northwest Alaska, took up the cause. They knew that the people of Kotzebue needed decent telephone service, and they wanted to help. Mauneluk filed a formal complaint with the APUC. The corporation asked the commission to revoke North State Telephone's "certificate of public convenience and necessity," its license to operate, or at least order North State Telephone to immediately improve its service. In its written complaint, Mauneluk told the commission that North State had failed to provide adequate service to the people of Kotzebue.

The complaint resulted in a formal case, officially called a "docket," before the commission. It was titled "North State

Telephone Company: Complaint of Mauneluk Association re Phone Service in Kotzebue." The case was opened in September 1974.[2]

The commission moved quickly. It was announced in November 1974 that the three APUC commissioners, led by Chairman Gordon Zerbetz, would travel to Kotzebue to hold a hearing about the service provided by North State Telephone. It was the first time in memory that the august state agency had held a hearing in our little town.

The hearing was held in the city council chambers on the second floor of Kotzebue's city hall. The chambers were really little more than a large empty room, but folding chairs and a folding table were set up from which the commissioners presided. More folding chairs were set up for the audience.

Unhappy telephone customers wrapped in winter gear arrived in large numbers. Once inside the building, they shed their big parkas. Ladies wearing *kuspuks* chattered in Inupiaq. The commissioners looked a bit uncomfortable as they began what was, for them, an unusual hearing.

But the formal hearing followed the commission's usual procedure. The commissioners heard testimony from anyone who wanted to speak. Each person was sworn in and then gave his or her name for the record.

To avoid the use of a telephone line — for obvious reasons — I had set up a radio link from the city hall to the KOTZ studio so that we could broadcast the hearing. People in Kotzebue and across northwest Alaska listened on the radio.

Mauneluk was represented by Alaska Legal Services lawyer Bob Bundy. He called several witnesses to testify, and each described problems with the service provided by North State. As reported in the *Kotzebue News*, the complaints included "extensive delays in getting a telephone installed in a residence or business, delayed dial tone, constantly being cut off during telephone conversations, and inoperable telephones for extended periods of time after damages to underground cables."[3]

Then I was called to testify.

The *Kotzebue News* reported:

> Alex Hills, testifying on behalf of Kotzebue Broadcasting, Inc. [KOTZ] … said that … an away Husky game being broadcast via long-distance had been deliberately interrupted by Mr. Gilbert, and Hills was able to document his statement. He also told the commission that when repairs are not made for many days the radio station is not able to receive news on the teletype or receive messages via telephone.[4]

A lady — one of Kotzebue's elders — testified in Inupiaq. Someone volunteered to translate for the commissioners. Others told about extended service outages. One spoke of an emergency medical situation in which a needed telephone wasn't working.[5]

When given his chance to testify, Mr. Gilbert said that

> He could not keep a full-time repairman in Kotzebue for the telephone exchange unless he received a rate increase [from the commission]. Mr. Gilbert, who lived in Anchorage, said he 'commuted' to do repair work in Kotzebue. The commission asked him if it would be possible for him to move to Kotzebue… Mr. Gilbert said that the commission could not force him to move here.[6]

The commissioners weren't impressed.

In the months that followed, APUC consumer affairs director Ray Wipperman told me about the commissioners' deliberations. He told me that it was unusual for the commission to revoke a utility's certificate. Legally they could do it, but they just didn't like the option.

Ray told me that the commissioners hoped that they could broker a sale of North State's Kotzebue property, equipment, and facilities to a local group able to take over the telephone operation. If such a deal could be negotiated, it would be, from their perspective, an easy way to settle things, and there would be no effect on North State's operations elsewhere in Alaska. But a new local phone company would be needed to make this plan work.

The commissioners didn't know that Kotzebue had been working on it. We were talking about forming a telephone cooperative, a nonprofit telephone company owned by its customers.

Electric and telephone cooperatives had been providing service to other parts of rural America for years. Beginning in the 1930s, the Rural Electrification Administration, a part of the U.S. Department of Agriculture, had extended low interest loans to facilitate the provision of electric power and telephone service, particularly in rural areas. The cooperatives typically served areas where profit-based companies were unwilling to provide service.

A telephone cooperative was just what the people of Kotzebue needed.

15

KOTZEBUE

MARCH 1975

A telephone cooperative could take over the North State system and make the improvements needed to upgrade Kotzebue's phone service. It would be a good first step, but I thought more was possible.

After improving Kotzebue's phone service, the same cooperative could be expanded to provide full telephone exchange service to all of the villages in our region. Every home and business in a village could have its own phone. The days of waiting in line to use a single village phone would be over. And the new village earth stations that were on the horizon could be used for long distance service.

But that project would have to wait a while. The first step was to improve Kotzebue's phone service.

Kotzebue's leading citizens had watched the North State situation unfold, and some of them were willing to get involved. A working group was formed by five of Kotzebue's leaders: James Gregg, George Conwell, Jerry Finke, Mabel Walsh, and Jeff

Knauer. All five were interested in creating a telephone cooperative.

But the new company would need a name.

Alaskans are air travelers and recognize airport designators, the three letter codes used to represent airports in Alaska, across the U.S., and around the world. The codes are the same three letters that appear on travelers' baggage tags. Some familiar ones are:

> LAX for Los Angeles International Airport,
>
> JFK for John F. Kennedy International Airport in New York City, and
>
> ORD for O'Hare Airport in Chicago.

In Alaska:

> ANC for Anchorage,
>
> FAI for Fairbanks,
>
> OME for Nome, and
>
> OTZ for Kotzebue.

Settling on Kotzebue's familiar airport designator, the working group quickly decided that the new company would be called the OTZ Telephone Cooperative.

At a March 1975 organizational meeting, Temporary President James Gregg described his negotiations with John Gilbert about the purchase price of the North State's Kotzebue equipment and facilities. At the meeting the group formally agreed that OTZ would "enter into a purchase agreement with North State Telephone Corporation to purchase the real and personal property pertaining to the telephone exchange and outside plant and equipment related thereto."[1]

The fledgling company was able to make the purchase only by using funds they borrowed from two local Native corporations. One was regional nonprofit corporation Mauneluk, and the other was NANA, the profit corporation for northwest Alaska. The loans were a big help, but the working group knew that they would have to later be repaid.

With approval of the working group, now called OTZ's temporary board of directors, the sale was completed. The APUC granted the new company a "certificate of public convenience and necessity," and the OTZ Telephone Cooperative officially became Kotzebue's telephone company. But the group knew that the company's equipment and outside plant were badly in need of upgrade and repair. A big job lay ahead.

The next step for the new cooperative was to hold a meeting of the general membership, the company's customer-owners, and elect a permanent board of directors. The meeting was set for 7 PM on Monday June 23, 1975.

54 people arrived at the big multipurpose room of the Kotzebue school. They drifted into the room, in ones, twos, and threes, chatting in English and Inupiaq. It was a big turnout for Kotzebue. The mood was upbeat. People hoped that their years of frustration with North State's telephone service were ending.

Temporary President James Gregg called the meeting to order and gave a quick summary of the formation of OTZ and its purchase of the North State facilities. Next came the election of the permanent board of directors. There were nominations from the floor and then a vote.

Five members were elected to the cooperative's first permanent board of directors: Al Adams, James Gregg, Tommy Sheldon, Nellie Ward, and me. All of the new board members had been involved, in one way or another, in the formation of OTZ. Nellie and I were known from our presence on the KOTZ airwaves and for our involvement in the basketball controversy. James Gregg and Tommy Sheldon were among the founders of OTZ, and Al Adams was a well-known local leader.[2]

Next on the agenda was approval of the cooperative bylaws that had been drafted by the temporary board. After some discussion, the bylaws were approved, and the general membership meeting ended with thanks to the temporary board members who had formed the new company.[3]

Then newly elected board members pulled folding chairs into a corner of the multipurpose room, where we convened our first board meeting. First we elected officers: I was elected President, James Gregg was Vice President, and Nellie Secretary/Treasurer. Nellie and I were glad to serve. At KOTZ we had experienced, more than most people, the difficulties caused by poor phone service.

I silently hoped that we would soon have satellite earth stations in all the villages and that the new cooperative would use the new earth stations to provide full telephone exchange service to people in the ten villages of our region. But more urgent matters were at hand, and our first board meeting moved on to the many details that were part of starting a new company.[4]

There was still lots of work to be done.

16

ANCHORAGE

JULY 1975

With the July agreement between RCA and the state complete, it was time for work on the new village earth stations to begin. Under the agreement, RCA was to install the earth stations at its own expense. This meant that the state's 5 million dollars would go farther than originally expected. Marv Weatherly decided to buy equipment for 120 — not 100 — earth stations. Twenty more villages than originally planned would be served by the new system.[1]

RCA's engineers and the state's engineers started working together to make the agreement a reality. Unlike their bosses, they worked well together. They were, after all, just doing a job. Two of them were John Lee, the civil engineer and pilot who had helped me with the bush telephone project, and University of Alaska electrical engineering professor Bob Merritt, who had designed antennas for the ATS-1 satellite demonstration project.

John Lee was still working with RCA, where he had become a key member of the company's technical team. Bob Merritt, still a professor and "dirty handed engineer," was an important member of the state's team.[2]

16-1 One of the 120 small earth stations destined for the villages.

The arguing was over. It was time for hard work, combined with practical engineering experience.

John's challenge was permafrost, permanently frozen ground, a serious problem in the north. It can lie anywhere from just a few inches below the ground's surface to several feet down. Scattered throughout northern Alaska, it gives engineers headaches.[3]

Foundations built over permafrost need to be specially designed. The danger is that the foundation will transfer heat to the ground and thaw the permafrost. When permafrost melts, the ground heaves, and the foundation can be damaged or destroyed. If the foundations of the new earth stations were not designed properly, melting permafrost could quickly throw the earth stations off kilter, and they would no longer be properly aimed at their target satellite.[4]

With his many years living and doing engineering work in rural Alaska, John was the right man to design foundations for the new village earth stations. He came up with a unique foundation for the earth station antennas, a foundation that was entirely above ground.[5]

John used big gabions — cages made of chicken wire — and filled them with sand bags. Each gabion was placed atop a 4-inch Styrofoam pad on the ground. This arrangement prevented heat from the foundation from disrupting the permafrost, and the sandbags provided the necessary weight, about 5 tons per gabion, to prevent the earth station's dish antenna from being moved around by high winds.[6]

Villagers helped to build the unusual foundation. They were, of course, happy to help with a project that would improve their communication with the outside world. The sandbags were covered with black polyethylene sheeting to prevent their canvas material from deteriorating under ultraviolet radiation from the sun. John's design worked well, and the foundations required little maintenance.[7]

In November, just five months after the agreement between RCA and the state, the first of the new village earth stations was finished. The 4.5 meter dish antenna was in place, resting on John's gabion foundation, and the equipment had been installed. The new earth station was ready to go.

It was in the small Inupiaq village of Noatak, 50 air miles north of Kotzebue. The people of Noatak, among KOTZ's most avid listeners, had followed the news about their new earth station by listening to the radio. They knew that their village would soon be part of Alaska's communication history.

A small ceremony was planned, but state officials, RCA executives, and other dignitaries found Noatak's weather forecast unappealing and decided not to make the trip. Only a small group of engineers and construction guys would be on hand for the event.

John Lee called me on the phone.

"We have to make a run up to Noatak to turn on that first earth station," he said. "Would you like to come along? I have an extra seat on the airplane."

16-2 Engineer and pilot John Lee at the controls.

A few days later John landed a silver and blue Cessna 180 on Kotzebue's long airstrip. Except for its color, the 180 looked much like our old red and white Cessna 185 with tail number 70022 — the one that had a few years earlier carried John and me to villages across Alaska.

Tom Henry, another RCA engineer, had flown into Kotzebue with Alaska Airlines the same day. When John landed, Tom and I were waiting. We jumped aboard the 180, and the three of us headed north to Noatak.

As we walked into the village, I spied the new earth station antenna. For me it was a welcome sight. It had been a long time coming.

Then I saw one of my old friends, a guy who had worked with John and me on the bush phone project. Ironworker Denver Carney waved a hello as he sat astride the dish antenna with a big wrench in his hand. With three of us together again, it was a reunion.

"This is like old home week," I said.

But the state officials and RCA executives who declined to make the Noatak trip had been right about November weather in the Arctic. The wind was starting to blow, and the aviation forecast predicted that flying weather would soon deteriorate. The earth station dedication ceremony was brief.

Afterward, John needed to finish a few more engineering tasks before leaving the village.

He suggested to Tom and me, "Why don't you fly with these two guys? They can drop you off in Kotzebue before they head back to Anchorage."

The "two guys" worked for the construction company that employed Denver to finish building the Noatak earth station antenna. I didn't catch their names.

So Tom and I climbed aboard their twin-engine Piper Comanche. The guy in the left front pilot's seat had won the plane in a poker game. He'd won it with a full house — three sevens and two kings, and that's why the plane's tail number was 777KK. I wondered if he was also lucky as a pilot.

His friend sat in the right front copilot's seat of the four-seater. Tom and I sat in the two rear seats. I'd been told that the guys in the front were both instrument-rated and well-experienced pilots.

As the Comanche gained altitude, the pilot established radio contact with the FAA flight service station in Kotzebue. The weather report we heard was bad. Through the static Kotzebue flight service reported "a quarter-mile visibility with strong winds, snow and blowing snow."

Another pilot had taken off from Noatak just behind us. When he heard the weather report, he told flight service he was "returning to Noatak to wait for better weather." That should have been a clue. But we headed toward Kotzebue.

As predicted, the weather got even worse. Soon Kotzebue flight service was reporting one-sixteenth of a mile visibility in snow and blowing snow. The pilot requested an instrument approach, but I thought he seemed a bit unsure. And the copilot seemed a little disoriented. We flew first in one direction and then another. I started to worry.

Soon Tom and I were looking down at ice floes and open water. Cold, open water. I guessed that we were somewhere west of Kotzebue over the Chukchi Sea. I looked at the two fuel gauges in the Comanche panel. Both were low. I gently suggested to the pilots it might be a good time to declare an emergency and request assistance from Kotzebue flight service. They ignored me

More minutes passed. More ice floes. More open water. The fuel gauges were dropping.

Finally, flight service asked the pilot "Would you like to request a DF steer, sir?"

Without waiting for response, the flight service specialist instructed the pilot to fly a heading directly toward the Kotzebue airport. After a time, he told the pilot to turn 90 degrees left, and 60 seconds later turn 90 degrees right, heading again toward the airport.

The flight service specialist on duty was using direction finding — DF — equipment that enabled him to read the direction of the aircraft measured from Kotzebue. This told him the direction the pilot should steer to head back to the airport. When the pilot turned 90 degrees left, the flight service specialist measured the change in the aircraft's direction from the airport over 60 seconds, and this allowed him to estimate the aircraft's distance from the airport.

More time passed. Flight service told us we were getting close to the airport.

I didn't know it at the time, but the Kotzebue fire department had lined up emergency vehicles riding on tank tracks at the edge of the Chukchi Sea. They were ready to race onto the sea ice to rescue us from the crash scene. They were not expecting a safe landing.

The flight service specialist's radio transmissions were becoming clearer:

"All souls on board maintain vigilance."

He wanted us to look for the airport and its runway lights.

I was the first to see the blue taxiway lights.

I shouted to the pilot, "The runway is there!"

I pointed down and to the right. I knew the airport layout.

The plane banked right. The runway lights came into view. The plane banked left and touched down on Kotzebue's long airstrip.

We landed safely! No scratches!

Without a word to the pilot or copilot, Tom and I jumped from the plane and walked to the Alaska Airlines terminal. We had nothing to say to them.

I called Meg to tell her I was okay.

She had been working at the hospital and said, "I didn't know there was a problem."

It was probably just as well.

The plane was soon refueled, and we found out that both tanks had been completely empty when we landed. We had been running on fumes.

The flight service specialist who guided us in later received a commendation from the FAA.

And the next day Meg and I celebrated Thanksgiving with friends.

17

KOTZEBUE

DECEMBER 1975

As Meg and I prepared to celebrate Christmas, I thought that, along with the people of our region, we had already received a great present. I took stock of things:

The new village earth stations were a success. At first each station offered two services: a single telephone and a "push-to-talk" medical channel used by village health aides to communicate with doctors in regional hospitals.[1]

Just as with RCA's earlier bush telephone program, one telephone was shared by all the people in a village. The satellite-based phones gave clear and steady service and were far more reliable than RCA's VHF system. Still, people needed to line up and wait to make a phone call.

Another thing hadn't changed. All phone calls from a village were long-distance calls and incurred long-distance charges. Each village needed someone to keep a log of the calls and be responsible for collecting money and paying the bill each month.

And there was a new wrinkle: satellite delay. Alaska's satellite was in orbit at 22,300 miles above the earth's surface. Signals traveled to and from the satellite at the speed of light, but it still took a quarter-second for a signal to travel from a village earth station through the satellite to another earth station. The quarter-second delay was noticeable.[2]

But it was really worse than that. A call placed from one village to another was switched at an exchange in Anchorage. This meant that a village caller's voice, when she called a friend in another village, would need to travel from her village earth station through the satellite to Anchorage — a quarter-second delay — and then from Anchorage back through the satellite to a friend in a second village — another quarter-second for a total half-second delay. That was really noticeable.

From the time the first villager asked her friend a question until she began to hear the friend's response, the delay was a full second, a half-second for her question to reach the friend, and another half-second for the friend's response to make the return trip. So a telephone caller perceived a full one second delay.

Everyone noticed it. It became a topic of conversation. During village-to-village phone calls, people interrupted each other, not knowing the right time to speak. Those with shortwave radio experience solved the problem by ending each statement or question with the word "over."

Still, these were minor problems. Having reliable and clear telephone service — even with satellite delay and a line of people waiting to make a call — was far better than poor service or no service at all.

The push-to-talk medical communication channel was used by village health aides. The health aides were offered a telephone-like service that would give each of them the opportunity to talk privately with a regional hospital doctor. But the health aides said they preferred the push-to-talk circuit. It was something like a party line, where everyone could hear what was said by others.

That was how their shortwave radios had been set up, and that was how they liked it.

The health aides said they wanted to listen to the doctors' advice to other health aides working in villages. They said there was educational value in hearing the doctors' advice to others. But they may have also liked the social network that the party line provided. The health aides, mostly women, were an informal sorority. They were a close knit group, and they liked to hear each other's voices on the satellite channel.

About a year, after the Noatak earth station was activated, a third satellite service was added, and it was a popular one. A single channel of entertainment television programming was transmitted to all the villages through the new earth stations. Low power transmitters like the ones used in the AEBC's mini-TV project were installed in the villages. The earlier project, which delivered programs by mailing videotapes, had inspired the satellite television system. But, with the new satellite hookup, programs were seen in the villages the same day they were seen in New York, Los Angeles, and Anchorage.[3] At first only 23 villages received television programs, but later the service was extended to include all villages with earth stations.

With same-day programming available in the villages, television salesmen began to arrive. They said the TV sets were selling better than *muktuk*.

But there was only one satellite channel to carry the entertainment television programming to the villages. They all received the same programs. There were three major commercial television networks — NBC, ABC, and CBS — and they all had popular programs. Three channels of television programming had to be whittled down to one channel to be broadcast to rural Alaska.

Who would decide which programs would be broadcast? Who would be willing to make decisions that were so important to village television fans? These were big decisions in rural Alaska, a place where people didn't like to make decisions that could offend others. No one wanted to be the bad guy.

And no politician or state bureaucrat was willing to make such sensitive and potentially unpopular decisions. It could have become a potential political football. So the state formed a committee of rural residents to make the decisions. The committee came to be called RATNET — the Rural Alaska Television Network — and the RATNET board included representatives from all regions of rural Alaska. Decisions were made by majority vote.

With its memorable name, RATNET became well-known across the state. For a time, the representative of Kotzebue and other communities in northwest Alaska was Nellie Ward, by then a beloved KOTZ radio broadcaster who could do no wrong in the eyes of her northwest Alaska constituents — even in the realm of television programming.

Still, each village had only one telephone. Waiting lines became longer and longer. I wanted the villages to have better phone service.

The new satellite earth stations could make it possible for each village to have its own telephone exchange — a "central office" in telephone parlance. With a village telephone exchange, telephone service would be available to every home and business in the village. Everyone could have a telephone.

This wasn't lost on the OTZ Telephone board members. By the time that first small earth station was installed in Noatak, we were already making plans.

18

KOTZEBUE

FEBRUARY 1976

Working with other OTZ Telephone board members, I put together a plan to provide service to the ten villages in our region: Buckland, Deering, Selawik, Noorvik, Kiana, Ambler, Shungnak, Kobuk, Noatak, and Kivalina. We thought we could provide phone service to every residence and business in the region by installing a telephone exchange in each village and connecting it to the new earth station. It would be groundbreaking. We would be the first company to use the new earth stations to provide full telephone service to rural Alaska.

But we needed the cooperation and approval of two government agencies to make it happen.

First, we would need a modified certificate from the APUC authorizing us to serve the ten villages. Then we would need funding to finance the village project. We hoped it would be in the form of a low interest loan from the federal Rural Electrification Administration — the REA.

We began to work with both agencies. In December we applied for a modified APUC certificate. Our application was formally established as an APUC case. The "docket" was opened and titled "OTZ Telephone Cooperative: Application to Extend Service Area."[1]

I didn't expect any problems with the commission because they had come to know us well, and they were impressed by the work we had done in taking over the Kotzebue telephone system.

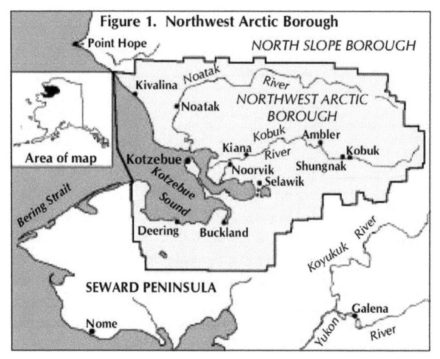

18-1 We planned to provide phone service to Kotzebue and the ten nearby villages of the region, now all part of the Northwest Arctic Borough.

We also started to work with the REA, and the agency assigned engineer Bob Peters to work with us. Bob traveled to Kotzebue to meet Nellie, me and others and to learn about our project. He was gracious, helpful, and extremely capable.

Bob and his engineer colleagues at the REA usually used microwave systems to interconnect telephone exchanges. It was the technology they knew, and it wasn't surprising that Bob talked about building a microwave system to interconnect Kotzebue and the villages. Small earth station technology was new and unfamiliar to the REA engineers. We would be the first anywhere to use them to interconnect small communities' telephone exchanges.

Microwave systems had already proven to be a troublesome way to connect Alaska villages. After I left RCA, the bush telephone project had tried to use microwave to extend the VHF radio phone system to villages that couldn't be served by VHF alone. The plan didn't go well. RCA's mountaintop relay stations used propane-fueled generators, which were refueled using helicopters. That was expensive. There were reliability problems — and an explosion at one of the mountaintop sites. I knew that microwave wasn't a good option — particularly with the new village earth stations being installed.

But microwave technology was familiar to Bob Peters and the engineers at REA, and they wanted to use it to interconnect our villages. I told Bob about the new satellite earth stations and explained that they would be a great way to interconnect our villages. He wasn't really interested.

We really needed the REA funding so I decided to play along with the microwave idea — at least for a while. It was a decision that would get me into trouble.

Our APUC and REA applications moved through their respective agencies — one state and one federal — in parallel. But, probably because of our previous work with the commission, our APUC application moved more quickly than the REA application.

Marv Weatherly and I were close. I admired Marv's courage, feistiness and persistence as he did battle with RCA. But during the summer of 1975 I could see that the stress was taking a toll. I suspected it was affecting Marv's health.

Marv talked to Governor Hammond about an opening on the APUC, and in August 1975 he was appointed to the vacant seat. It was a good decision. As a commissioner Marv would be able to continue his involvement in building and improving Alaska's telecommunication system, but he would be a step removed from the front lines of battle. There would be less stress.

With Marv moving to a new job, consultant Bob Walp, who had been at Marv's side at that contentious lunch with Stephen Heller, became the new director of Gov. Hammond's Office of Telecommunications. Bob picked up the small satellite earth station project where Marv had left off.

In March 1976 the APUC commissioners traveled to Kotzebue for a hearing that was, in a way, a repeat of their November 1974 visit. We already had a certificate authorizing us to serve Kotzebue, but this time the commissioners would hold a hearing on the application to our extend service area to include the ten villages in our region.

The commission's membership had changed since the 1974 hearing. Gordon Zerbetz was still the chairman, but the other commissioners were new. Two spots on the commission were reserved for an engineer and an attorney. Gov. Hammond had appointed Marv as the engineer commissioner and Stuart Hall as the attorney commissioner.

And in its 1975 session, the Alaska legislature had added two additional seats to the commission. Both were consumer seats intended to represent all Alaskans. Carolyn Guess and Susan Knowles had been appointed as the new consumer commissioners.

Four of the five commissioners, Gordon, Marvin, Carolyn and Susan, showed up for the hearing that day. The fifth commissioner, Stuart Hall, didn't make the trip.

The commissioners again arrived in Kotzebue aboard an Alaska Airlines jet. There was lots of snow on the ground, and I met the commissioners at the airport pulling a long sled with my snow machine. I bundled them into the sled for the short trip to Kotzebue city hall.

Three commissioners, Marv, Carolyn, and Susan, rode in the basket of the sled, but Gordon insisted on "riding runners." He stood at the back of the sled — on its runners — hanging on tightly. He may have imagined that he was running Alaska's new sled dog race, the Iditarod, which was suddenly famous across America. But he was being pulled by my snow machine — not by sled dogs. For the four commissioners, the sled ride seemed to be an adventure.

18-2 I bundled the commissioners into my sled and drove them to Kotzebue's city hall.

I drove slowly, delivering the four VIPs to the city hall safely and without incident. I knew that even a small accident wouldn't help our chances to get the certificate we needed.

People were curious as they trickled into the city council chambers. Again, ladies wearing *kuspuks* took their seats. And Meg arrived, too, with our new baby daughter Becky concealed in her parka. It was a cold day. Meg had decided to *umuk* the baby, carrying her inside a big, oversize parka. Arriving in the hearing room, Meg loosened the leather strap around the parka's waist, and caught baby Becky as she dropped off her mother's back. The locals in the room noticed nothing unusual, but the four commissioners' eyes opened wide.

This time most of the people hoping to benefit from the hearing's outcome were not in the room. They were at home in the villages, listening to the broadcast on KOTZ.

The hearing was going well until I was called to testify. Commissioner Marv was, of course, well informed about the progress of the small earth stations being installed under the RCA-state program, and he questioned me closely about the technical details of our plan to extend full phone service to the villages. At one point Marv heard the word "microwave," and his eyes narrowed.

Then things went downhill.

After I finished my direct testimony, Marv's first question was:

"Do you mean to tell me that you're planning to install a <u>microwave</u> system to interconnect villages that are receiving small satellite earth stations?"

I shifted in my chair.

"Commissioner, we are in discussions with the REA about funding our new village program, and the REA engineers are most familiar with using microwave to interconnect central offices."

Marv asked again:

"Do you mean to tell me that you're planning to install a <u>microwave</u> system to interconnect the villages?"

His voice was rising.

"Commissioner, I've been working with REA to explain to them the advantages of using the new satellite system. I'm optimistic that they will ultimately see the light on this."

Marv came back:

"Well, they better see the light, or this project goes nowhere."

"Yes sir," I responded.

The other commissioners were silent.

There were no further questions.

My optimism was rewarded when we later convinced REA that the new satellite system would avoid the problems of refueling and accessing microwave repeater stations under difficult Arctic conditions. Also, the state and RCA were committed to investing in the earth stations, and their investment would, to some extent, be wasted if we duplicated it with a separate microwave system.

Our REA application was soon approved. We would use the new satellite system to interconnect the villages. Our APUC application was also approved. Our service area now included all eleven communities in our region — Kotzebue and the ten villages.

With the APUC and REA approvals behind us, things started to move quickly. In the summer of 1976 we hired Philip Day as our general manager, and we hired former KOTZ announcer Joe Hill to oversee construction of the new "central office" buildings that would hold our telephone exchange equipment in the villages. Since the days he worked as an announcer at KOTZ, Joe had become a skilled carpenter and builder known throughout the region. We were happy to have him on the new project.

By the fall of 1976 things were really humming. We had a permanent general manager, staff including two installers, and an office manager. Our planning for the new village telephone exchanges was underway

OTZ Telephone was on the path to providing full and reliable telephone service to the residents of northwest Alaska — telephone service that was made possible by those small satellite earth stations that Augie Hiebert, Bob Merritt, Marv Weatherly, and others had championed.

EPILOGUE

Soon after that first earth station was installed in Noatak, other villages began to receive their own earth stations, and within a few years, 120 villages had earth stations. More villages would get earth stations later. Like OTZ Telephone Cooperative, other local exchange companies began to install telephone exchanges in villages, using them with the earth stations to provide local and long-distance telephone service to village customers.

In rare cases long-distance telephone service had previously been available to the villages without the use of satellite communications, and there were a few companies that provided telephone service using these connections. But the new earth stations opened up telephone service to many more villages and small communities spread all across Alaska.

While OTZ was the first telephone company to connect a local exchange to a village earth station, other companies began to do the same. Among these were:

> Arctic Slope Telephone Association Cooperative, serving the villages across the north slope of Alaska,

> Bristol Bay Telephone Cooperative, serving villages in the Bristol Bay area,

> Nushagak Electric and Telephone Cooperative, serving the villages in the Dillingham area,

> Bush-Tell, serving interior villages along the Yukon and Kuskokwim rivers,

Interior Telephone Company, serving villages scattered all across the state,

Mukluk Telephone Company, serving the villages on the Seward Peninsula and around Norton Sound,

United Utilities, serving villages across a broad area of southwest Alaska, and

Yukon Telephone Company, serving a few villages in the interior and along the Alaska's southcentral coast.

After RCA bought the Alaska Communications System from the U.S. Air Force in 1971, and after they tangled with Alaska's state government, the company eventually made a major commitment to the use of satellite technology in its network, and, for years, satellite technology was a big part of Alaska's telecommunication story. In 1979 Pacific Power and Light, through its subsidiary Pacific Telecom, purchased RCA Alascom, then simply called it Alascom, Inc. In 1995 the company was again sold, this time to AT&T. It is now known as AT&T Alascom.

In 1982 RCA began to launch a series of communication satellites that served Alaska for many years. The first was named Aurora I, and it was dedicated exclusively to Alaska service. Two more satellites were later launched, Aurora II in 1991, and Aurora III in 2000, also dedicated to serving Alaska. At this writing (in 2016), Aurora III continues to provide service to Alaska.

While AT&T Alascom still provides long-distance telephone service and other long-haul communication throughout Alaska, it now has competition in this market, notably from General Communication Inc. — GCI — based in Anchorage. But RCA remains Alaska's "carrier of last resort," which means it is obligated to provide service to communities in Alaska that GCI and other carriers don't serve.

Many more radio stations joined the airwaves to serve rural Alaska villages. Like KOTZ, some use the AM band to serve huge coverage areas.

The first public radio station in rural Alaska was Bethel's KYUK, which signed on in 1971. (The only earlier public radio station in Alaska was KUAC at the University of Alaska in Fairbanks — then Alaska's second largest city and not really part of rural Alaska.) Kotzebue's KOTZ was the second rural public radio station, and, as you've read, it signed on in 1973.

After KOTZ was running smoothly, I helped Dillingham's KDLG and Barrow's KBRW get started. Both stations signed on in 1975, and more stations soon followed, including KMXT Kodiak, KRBD Ketchikan, KSTK Wrangell, and KFSK Petersburg, which used FM frequencies to cover smaller areas but deliver FM's higher sound quality to their listeners. I also helped to build Nome's KNOM, which signed on in 1971. While it was not a member of the public radio community, the Catholic-owned station provided many of the same services as its public radio brethren.

In 1978 I was asked to become the founding general manager of Anchorage public radio station KSKA, and the station signed on in the same year. Because the need for radio broadcast stations in the far reaches of Alaska was so great, much of rural Alaska had public radio service before Anchorage, Alaska's largest city.

The state's public radio stations banded together in 1978 to form the Alaska Public Radio Network, which has produced and distributed programs of statewide interest to its member stations across the state for the past 38 years. In those same years, many more public radio stations have joined the airwaves. Today Alaska has 25 public radio stations.

By the mid-1980s most Alaska villages had what were then modern telecommunication services: radio broadcast service, television broadcast service, full local exchange telephone service, and at least a two-way circuit for medical communication.

On the other hand, in the decades that followed, Internet service was slow to arrive in the villages. But today a new generation of technology pioneers is working on solving that problem.

It might someday be the subject of another book.

ABBREVIATIONS

ABA: Alaska Broadcasters Association

ACS: Alaska Communications System

AEBC: Alaska Educational Broadcasting Commission, later renamed Alaska Public Broadcasting Commission (APBC)

Alascom: Refers to RCA Alaska Communications, Inc. Its successor companies were Alascom owned by Pacific Telecom, and AT&T Alascom, owned by AT&T

APUC: Alaska Public Utilities Commission, which was later renamed the Regulatory Commission of Alaska (RCA)

AT&T: American Telephone and Telegraph Company

COMSAT: Communications Satellite Corporation

DF: direction finding

FAA: Federal Aviation Administration

FCC: Federal Communications Commission

NANA: NANA Regional Corporation, the regional for-profit Native Corporation for northwest Alaska

OTZ: OTZ Telephone Cooperative, Inc., named for the Kotzebue, Alaska airport identifier

RATNET: Rural Alaska Television Network

RCA Alascom: RCA Alaska Communications, Inc.

RCA: Radio Corporation of America

REA: Rural Electrification Administration, which was later renamed the Rural Utilities Service (RUS)

UHF: Ultra high frequency, 300 to 3000 MHz

VHF: Very high frequency, 30 to 300 MHz

PHOTO CREDITS

FOREWORD SUPPLEMENT

An expanded version of the book's Foreword:

Alaska's telecommunication systems have been built — or attempted to be built — by colorful characters, smart people and innovators who've changed the world. Success has also depended on working well with families who have lived in Alaska for 10,000 years — Alaska Natives — who have welcomed new connections across this vast, cold, place, but who, often in the same breath, want to be sure that their own languages and customs are preserved and protected.

I've worked with some of those colorful, innovative characters who are also heroes of this book. University of Alaska professor Bob Merritt and I were in a wireless venture with GCI cofounder Ron Duncan, former Lt. Governor Terry Miller and a larger cast of characters in the early 1980's. Bob was a guy who could invent a new antenna in his lab, and install it by climbing a tower in the hills near Fairbanks at 40 below, all while maintaining his impish trademark smile, even at four in the morning. Augie Hiebert, who built radio and television stations in Alaska, offered me a job, when I was just out of high school, as a weekend anchorman. (My mother reminded me I had to go to college instead.) Augie promoted small satellite earth stations as ideal for Alaska's challenges, and he made sure that the Bartlett earth station was working in time to carry live coverage of the first moon landing to Alaska in 1969. (I later ran into Augie at Anchorage's railroad station, where he was escorting another anchorman, Walter Cronkite, who had narrated CBS coverage of the moon landing.)

For the past 150 years or so, there's almost always been someone — for motives of national strategy or profit or both— trying to string cables across Alaska. Telegraph, telephone, television, fiber optic and data technologies continue to improve our ability to communicate. Communication cables, actual and proposed, have come, would have come, or will come by land and sea — across the Pacific from Asia, up from North America through the Yukon to cross the Bering Strait to Russia and Europe, or even, as recently proposed, across the fabled Northwest Passage, to link Tokyo and London.

Fiber optic cables today link our Arctic oilfields with control rooms in Houston; our missile defense launch sites and radars with command centers in Colorado Springs; and our offices, homes, libraries, clinics and classrooms to the planet's central nervous system, the Internet. Communication systems before that, some with cables, some without, linked our listening posts in the Bering Sea and the Aleutian Islands to the Pentagon. Alaskans can be proud that airmen listening to Russian signals from Shemya, near the end of the Aleutian Islands, predicted the Soviet launch of Sputnik, mankind's first satellite, in 1957. The same airmen later confirmed it.[1]

Since Sputnik and the dawn of the space age, Alaska has had a variety of satellites overhead: in special polar orbits to drop geographic data into big dishes in Fairbanks, or in low-earth orbiting constellations operating as mesh networks that pass voice and data communications bird-to-bird, ready to pick up or drop off transmissions anywhere on the planet. Even satellites far to the south of us, sitting 22,300 miles above the equator get into the act — providing a link for calls between Alaska villages.

If wires and satellites aren't enough, we've also dotted the landscape with antennae big and small, some powered by radioisotope thermal generators to sense Russian nuclear tests, some as big as drive-in movie theater screens, and all busying the airways with high frequency, very high frequency, or microwave communication. Ground-breaking technology developed by one of our three big telecom firms, GCI, drastically reduced the capital cost for bringing mobile phone systems to rural communities in Alaska.[2] And our state government got directly into the act, spending hundreds of millions of dollars on its own land mobile radio system, subsidizing the proliferation of television signals across the state, and helping to sustain public radio in parts of Alaska that would not afford it otherwise.

Throughout this history, there have been some common themes:

First, Alaska is a proving ground. Geosynchronous satellites were proposed by my favorite science fiction writer, Arthur C. Clarke, a signalman and radar operator in the British Armed Forces in World War II. Clarke, in a letter published in *Wireless World* in 1945, suggested the use of the 36,000 km orbit which now bears his name, for global telecommunications. Writing in the era of the German V-2 rocket attacks, Clarke predicted it might take 40-50 years to achieve, but it happened sooner than that — in time to put live television coverage of the 1964 Tokyo Olympics in America's living rooms, as well as same-day coverage of the horrors of the Vietnam War. Alaska became a major user of geosynchronous satellites in rural communities in the 1970's and 1980's; we led the world in the application of small earth stations, small autonomous cell systems, public Wi-Fi, meteor-trail signal bounces, and other emerging technologies.[3]

A second theme in Alaska telecom history has been intense competition. Competitors often battle for subsidies, mind share and market share, especially when one technology or communication route is poised to replace another. Things got so intense in the 1980's as GCI challenged incumbents ATT Alascom and local telephone companies that the time is remembered as "phone wars." Even the proposed telegraph line across Alaska in the 1860's competed against the trans-Atlantic cable, which ultimately won. Today satellites and fiber battle microwave for position as the best way to serve rural Alaska. Within these worlds, Alaskans are often asked to take sides, where the perfect is posed as "the enemy of the good," or where old technology is hailed for its reliability, and new technology is questioned about its ability to keep its promises. Now, as fiber optic cables are being laid to connect our Arctic coastal communities, naysayers are warning that ice scour in the Bering, Chukchi and Beaufort Seas is likely to chop those lines.

A third common theme in this history of Alaska telecommunications is that we've tended to attract some colorful, hardy, visionary and inventive characters. Folks who regularly climb towers at 40 below are a special breed. Few governors in America have shared their Alaska colleagues' experience of committing large sums of money to satellite systems that were once thought impossible. Leaders in corporate boardrooms here, as everywhere, are constantly ready to prove once again that capitalism is, as MIT economist Joseph Schumpeter put it, "creative destruction." We are innovators by necessity, and our laboratories are hardly comfortable. Northern telecommunications are challenged not just by cold, dark and distance, but the radiation that causes the *aurora borealis*, which can sap reliability in an instant.[4]

The fourth theme in Alaska's telecom history is that Alaskans themselves have consistently welcomed improvements. Some Alaskans are proud to be "off the grid," but many want the benefits of living out where the resources are — fish, game, minerals, etc. — but with the benefit of being in touch, not just to order supplies or a medevac but also to pursue family life when families are separated.

Before telegraph and telephones, we relied on ships at sea, runners on land, blazes or cairns on trails, and perhaps smoke signals to get messages across distances to each other. Trading spots, like

Yukon Island in Kachemak Bay, became a crossroads for communication between various cultures in our state. At close range, given that written communication did not exist here before the Russians' 1741 arrival, Alaskans communicated with talk, dance and song. (Now we are working to preserve language and culture, using some of the same telecommunications tools that have put pressure on the use of traditional languages in Alaska.)

This new book by Alex Hills amplifies all of these themes. After serving in Korea as a U.S. military officer, Alex arrived in Alaska and soon found himself in the state's "phone wars." But he has consistently been on the side of advancing technology — sometimes finding ways to make old technology work and sometimes helping to create new technology. He has encountered life-threatening challenges and ornery bureaucrats with the sense of humor displayed in these pages. He has, again and again, been in uncomfortable situations and come out with innovation.

Alex came to Alaska with the perspective that anything is possible if you keep working the problem. He puts no limits on his thinking, and he uses his imagination. He's as comfortable in a Silicon Valley boardroom as climbing a tower in Bethel or leading his students to a remote part of the world — Malawi in southern Africa or an Amazon jungle town in Peru, for example.

When I first met Alex I wasn't surprised to find that an Alaskan had led the team that built the first large Wi-Fi network. Since then I've worked with Alex in several settings: as a member of the Alaska Science and Technology Foundation Board in the late 1990's, developing a wireless location-based technology at Venture Ad Astra, establishing the Alaska Innovator's Hall of Fame, and now serving with him on Iridium's Polar Advisory Board, where we're helping to build a global satellite network to help solve problems in the north.

Reading this book told me more about Alex than I'd learned over coffee in the last 20 years, and helps me understand the human element behind our phone systems, more than any other account of telecommunications in Alaska. Now I'll be sure I don't take for granted that phone call to rural Alaska — ever!

Mead Treadwell[5]
Anchorage, Alaska

SOURCES

"APUC Hears Public." *Kotzebue News*, November 23, 1974.

Alaska Public Utilities Commission Docket U-74-091.

Alaska Public Utilities Commission Docket U-75-099.

Chlupach, Robin Ann, *Airwaves over Alaska: The Story of Broad-caster Augie Hiebert*. Issaquah, WA: Sammamish Press, 1992.

Heller, Stephen D., letter to Alex Hills, Anchorage, Alaska, July 30, 1973.

Heller, Stephen D., letter to Alex Hills, Anchorage, Alaska, May 13, 1973.

Heller, Stephen D., letter to Alex Hills, Anchorage, Alaska, November 28, 1973.

Heller, Stephen D., letter to Alex Hills, Anchorage, Alaska, October 8, 1973.

Hills, Alex, "Alaska's Giant Satellite Network." *IEEE Spectrum*, July 1983, pp. 50-55.

Hills, Alex, "Melting the Ice Curtain between Russia and Alaska." *Business Communications Review*, December 1993, pp. 26-29.)

Hills, Alex, "Subzero Engineering." *IEEE Spectrum*, December 1986, pp. 52-56.

Hills, Alex, "Our Public Relations Problems in the Villages," memorandum, December 22, 1972.

Hills, Alex, letter to Stephen D. Heller, Anchorage, Alaska, June 25, 1973.

Hills, Alex, letter to Stephen D. Heller, Kotzebue, Alaska, August 27, 1973.

Hills, Alex, letter to Stephen D. Heller, Kotzebue, Alaska, May 6, 1974.

Hills, Alex, letter to Stephen D. Heller, Kotzebue, Alaska, November 19, 1973.

Hills, Alex, *Wi-Fi and the Bad Boys of Radio: Dawn of a Wireless Technology*. Indianapolis, IN: Dog Ear Publishing, 2011.

Hudson, Heather E., *Connecting Alaskans: Telecommunications in Alaska from Telegraph to Broadband*. Fairbanks, AK: University of Alaska Press, 2015.

Merritt, R.P., "The Alaska Telecommunication System." *The Northern Engineer*, winter 1981, University of Alaska Geophysical Institute, Fairbanks, Alaska.

Millsap, Pam, "Hickel Raps Egan and RCA," *Anchorage Daily News*, June 28, 1974, as quoted in Hudson, Heather E., *Connecting Alaskans: Telecommunications in Alaska from Telegraph to Broadband*. Fairbanks, AK: University of Alaska Press, 2015. p. 101.

"Minutes of the Meeting of the Temporary Board of Directors of the OTZ Telephone Cooperative Inc.," March 27, 1975.

"Minutes of the Organizational Meeting of the OTZ Telephone Cooperative, Inc.," June 23, 1975.

"Minutes of the Regular Meeting of the Board of Directors of the OTZ Telephone Cooperative," June 23-24, 1975.

Personal communication, Lee Wareham, January 2016.

Personal communication, Nellie and Gregory Moore, January 2016.

Southeast Alaska Empire, May 4, 1972, as reported in Chlupach, *Airwaves Over* Alaska, 163.

Walp, Robert M., "First Hand: C-Band Story," as quoted in Hudson, *Connecting Alaskans*, 108.

Weatherly, Marvin, interview with Hilary Hilscher, December 26, 2000.

NOTES

Chapter 1

1. In the 1970s, when this story takes place, the Native people of northern and western Alaska were commonly called "Eskimos." More recently, the term has been criticized by some, but in the 1970s Alaskans said "Eskimo." Within this large group are the Inupiaq people of the north and northwest parts of Alaska, the Yup'ik people of western Alaska, the Alutiiq people of southwest Alaska, and the Siberian Yup'ik people of St. Lawrence Island in the Bering Sea. In this book the terms Inupiaq, Yup'ik, Alutiiq, and Siberian Yup'ik are used as appropriate.

2. The people Alaskans commonly call "Indians" include a number of distinct tribes whose languages are more closely related to the Native tribes of Canada and the South 48. These include the Athabascans of Alaska's interior, the Tlingit, Tsimshian, and Haida Indians of the southeast Alaska panhandle, and the Eyak of the Prince William Sound area.

3. Alaska's vast size and scattered population heightened the importance of telecommunications services but also intensified the difficulty of providing them. The state spans about 1500 miles from north to south and over 2500 miles from east to west. In 1972 Alaska had only a little more than 300,000 people, and 16 per cent of them were Alaska Natives, many living in the hundreds of small villages scattered across the state.

Alaska has three mountain ranges, the highest peak in North America — Denali, about 20,300 feet high — and the longest North American River — the Yukon, close to 1800 miles long. The land varies from the flat tundra of the northwest to the heavily forested mountainous areas of the southeast that are interrupted by a multitude of fjords.

4. This book's descriptions of our work on the "bush telephone program" are drawn in many cases from a log that I kept from June 1972 to May 1973.

5. Throughout most of the twentieth century, most of the nation's phone service was provided by the American Telephone and Telegraph Company — AT&T — which operated the Bell telephone companies. Back then many familiarly referred to this collection of companies as "Ma Bell."

6. The best location for our equipment and antenna was one with a direct radio path to a base station that could be connected to the existing telephone network. VHF signals travel a direct line from a transmitting to a receiving antenna. In each village we looked for a "clear shot" to the nearest base station.

There were complications, though. One was shadowing. A physical obstruction might block or partially block a signal's direct path. A bush telephone signal could penetrate the walls of a wood frame house, but, because of the shadowing effect, it would be weaker inside the house. That's why we used antennas mounted outside the buildings.

Terrain features, like nearby hills and mountains, could cause more serious shadowing. A VHF signal of any frequency had little chance of penetrating a mountain. We always used outdoor antennas mounted high enough to avoid the shadowing caused by obstructions like hills, mountains and nearby buildings.

Another problem was reflection. When a transmitted VHF signal encounters a smooth, flat surface, especially a metallic surface, it can be reflected, just as a light ray is reflected from a mirror. We considered VHF reflections to be a bad thing. Reflections off the ground and the surfaces of lakes and rivers could cause problems when, at the receiver, the reflected signal was recombined with the direct signal. There were other more subtle effects called refraction, scattering and diffraction. All of these are described in: Hills, Alex, *Wi-Fi and the Bad Boys of Radio: Dawn of a Wireless Technology*. Indianapolis, IN: Dog Ear Publishing, 2011.

Chapter 2

1. *Ulu* is the name most commonly used for this knife in Alaska, but this is actually a word in Inupiaq, the language of northwest and north Alaska. In the Cup'ik, dialect spoken in Scammon Bay, an *ulu* is called a *kegginalek*. Cup'ik is a dialect of the Yup'ik language.

2. The Inupiaq word for "Eskimo ice cream" is *akutaq*.

3. Hills, Alex, "Alaska's Giant Satellite Network." *IEEE Spectrum*, July 1983, pp. 50-55.

4. Hudson, Heather E., *Connecting Alaskans: Telecommunications in Alaska from Telegraph to Broadband*. Fairbanks, AK: University of Alaska Press, 2015. p. 57.

5. Before RCA bought the system, Alaska's long-distance telephone traffic had been carried on the Air Force's Alaska Communication System — the ACS. The system was operated primarily for military purposes, but, since it was the only system available, the Air Force also permitted some civilian long-distance traffic on the network. The ACS system relied heavily on microwave and cable links, supplemented by the so-called White Alice Communication System, a UHF "tropospheric scatter" system built in the 1950s.

But Alaskans were not satisfied with ACS services. In 1968 Congress authorized the sale of the system to a private entity after bids were solicited. RCA was the successful bidder. As part of its agreement to purchase the ACS, RCA made a commitment to provide telephone service to 142 villages, explore the use of satellite communications in 49 locations, and invest more than $28 million to upgrade the system. RCA set up a subsidiary, RCA Alaska Communications, Inc. — RCA Alascom — to operate the network.

Chapter 3

1. Hills, Alex, "Our Public Relations Problems in the Villages," memorandum, December 22, 1972.

2. Ibid.

3. Ibid.

4. Ibid.

5. These big antennas were used by the military's Cold War era White Alice Communication System. It used UHF tropospheric scatter technology.

Chapter 4

1. Chlupach, Robin Ann, *Airwaves Over Alaska: The Story of Broadcaster Augie Hiebert*. Issaquah, WA: Sammamish Press, 1992. pp. 18-20.

2. Ibid., p. 22.

3. Ibid., pp. 21- 22.

4. Ibid., pp. 23-24.

5. Ibid., p. 34.

6. "Rhombus" is the geometric name for a four sided figure, all of whose sides have the same length.

7. Ibid., pp. 37-38.

8. Ibid., p. 38.

9. Ibid., p. 41.

10. Ibid., pp. 41-42.

11. Ibid.

12. Ibid., pp. 47-48.

13. Ibid., pp. 126-131.

14. Ibid.

15. The Alaska Broadcasters Association now has a broader mission, but it's still a vital broadcaster's organization.

16. Hudson, Heather E., *Connecting Alaskans: Telecommunications in Alaska from Telegraph to Broadband*. Fairbanks, AK: University of Alaska Press, 2015. pp. 70-71.

17. Chlupach, *Airwaves Over* Alaska, 137.

18. Ibid., pp. 133-136.

Chapter 5

1. Hudson, Heather E., *Connecting Alaskans: Telecommunications in Alaska from Telegraph to Broadband*. Fairbanks, AK: University of Alaska Press, 2015. pp. 79-81.

2. Ibid.

3. Ibid.

4. Ibid.

Chapter 6

1. Hills, Alex, "Subzero Engineering." *IEEE Spectrum*, December 1986, pp. 52-56.

2. Ibid.

3. Hills, Alex, "Melting the Ice Curtain between Russia and Alaska." *Business Communications Review*, December 1993, pp. 26-29.

4. Ibid.

5. Ibid.

6. Ibid.

7. Ibid.

8. Ibid.

9. Ibid.

10. Hills, Alex, "Subzero Engineering," 52-56.

11. Ibid.

12. Ibid.

13. Ibid.

14. Ibid.

15. Hills, Alex, letter to Stephen D. Heller, Anchorage, Alaska, June 25, 1973.

16. Ibid.

17. Ibid.

18. Ibid.

19. Ibid.

20. Ibid.

Chapter 7

1. They're called "snowmobiles" in most of the United States, but in Alaska they're "snow machines."

2. Chlupach, Robin Ann, *Airwaves Over Alaska: The Story of Broadcaster Augie Hiebert*. Issaquah, WA: Sammamish Press, 1992. p. 106.

Chapter 8

1. Heller, Stephen D., letter to Alex Hills, Anchorage, Alaska, July 30, 1973.

2. Ibid.

3. Ibid.

4. Hills, Alex, letter to Stephen D. Heller, Kotzebue, Alaska, August 27, 1973.

5. Ibid.

6. Heller, Stephen D., letter to Alex Hills, Anchorage, Alaska, October 8, 1973.

Chapter 9

1. Personal communication, Nellie and Gregory Moore, January 2016.

2. Ibid.

3. Ibid.

4. Ibid.

5. Ibid.

6. Ibid.

7. Ibid.

8. Ibid.

9. Ibid.

10. Chlupach, Robin Ann, *Airwaves Over Alaska: The Story of Broadcaster Augie Hiebert*. Issaquah, WA: Sammamish Press, 1992. p. 154-155.

11. Personal communication, Lee Wareham, January 2016.

12. Ibid.

13. Ibid.

14. Ibid.

15. Ibid.

16. Ibid.

17. Ibid.

18. Ibid.

19. Chlupach, *Airwaves Over* Alaska, 162.

20. Ibid. pp. 161-164.

21. Ibid.

22. Ibid.

23. Hudson, Heather E., *Connecting Alaskans: Telecommunications in Alaska from Telegraph to Broadband*. Fairbanks, AK: University of Alaska Press, 2015. pp. 71- 74.

24. Ibid.

25. *Southeast Alaska Empire*, May 4, 1972, as reported in Chlupach, *Airwaves Over* Alaska, 163.

26. Chlupach, *Airwaves Over* Alaska 161-164.

27. Hudson, *Connecting* Alaskans, 74.

Chapter 10

1. A hooded overgarment traditionally worn by Native men and women.

2. Later Nellie Ward became Nellie Moore, Alaska's leading native journalist.

3. Hills, Alex, letter to Stephen D. Heller, Kotzebue, Alaska, November 19, 1973.

4. Ibid.

5. Heller, Stephen D., letter to Alex Hills, Anchorage, Alaska, November 28, 1973.

Chapter 12

1. Chlupach, Robin Ann, *Airwaves Over Alaska: The Story of Broadcaster Augie Hiebert*. Issaquah, WA: Sammamish Press, 1992. pp.154-155.

2. Robert Sarnoff was chairman of the RCA Corporation.

3. Hills, Alex, letter to Stephen D. Heller, Kotzebue, Alaska, May 6, 1974.

4. Heller, Stephen D., letter to Alex Hills, Anchorage, Alaska, May 13, 1974.

Chapter 13

1. Millsap, Pam, "Hickel Raps Egan and RCA," *Anchorage Daily News*, June 28, 1974, as quoted in Hudson, Heather E., *Connecting Alaskans: Telecommunications in Alaska from Telegraph to Broadband*. Fairbanks, AK: University of Alaska Press, 2015. p. 101.

2. Merritt, R.P., "The Alaska Telecommunication System." *The Northern Engineer*, Winter 1981, University of Alaska Geophysical Institute, Fairbanks, Alaska.

3. Hudson, *Connecting* Alaskans, 80-81.

4. Ibid. pp. 102-106.

5. Ibid. p. 101.

6. Ibid. pp. 107-108.

7. Ibid.

8. Walp, Robert M., "First Hand: C-Band Story," as quoted in Hudson, *Connecting Alaskans*, 108.

9. Ibid.

10. Ibid.

11. Ibid.

12. Ibid.

13. Hudson, *Connecting Alaskans*, 109.

14. Weatherly, Marvin, interview with Hilary Hilscher, December 26, 2000.

15. Ibid.

16. Hudson, *Connecting Alaskans*, 116.

17. Ibid.

Chapter 14

1. The name of the nonprofit corporation is now spelled "Maniilaq," but in 1974 and 1975 the spelling was "Mauneluk."

2. Alaska Public Utilities Commission Docket U-74-091.

3. "APUC Hears Public." *Kotzebue News*, November 23, 1974.

4. Ibid.

5. Ibid.

6. Ibid.

Chapter 15

1. "Minutes of the Meeting of the Temporary Board of Directors of the OTZ Telephone Cooperative Inc.," March 27, 1975.

2. "Minutes of the Organizational Meeting of the OTZ Telephone Cooperative, Inc.," June 23, 1975.

3. Ibid.

4. "Minutes of the Regular Meeting of the Board of Directors of the OTZ Telephone Cooperative," June 23-24, 1975.

Chapter 16

1. Hills, Alex, "Subzero Engineering." *IEEE Spectrum*, December 1986, pp. 54-55.

2. Ibid.

3. Ibid.

4. Ibid.

5. Ibid.

6. Ibid.

7. Ibid.

Chapter 17

1. Hills, Alex, "Alaska's Giant Satellite Network." *IEEE Spectrum*, July 1983, p.53.

2. Ibid. p.52.

3. Ibid. pp. 54-55.

Chapter 18

1. Alaska Public Utilities Commission Docket U-75-099.

Foreword Supplement

1. Clarence Smith, a business partner of mine at Venture Ad Astra, which — among other things — invested in the 360 degree camera which pioneered Google's Street View, was head of Shemya's listening post at the time. Smith became one of the first employees in the CIA's Science and Technology Division, and went on to play a major role in our nation's reconnaissance satellite program. I hope someday to read his classified history of the National Reconnaissance Office.

2. Gene Strid, vice president and chief engineer of network services at General Communications Corp (GCI) was recognized in the first class of the Alaska Innovators Hall of Fame for that invention, as was the author of this book, Alex Hills, for his pioneering work on another technology used worldwide, called Wi-Fi.

3. Clarke wrote in 1945 in *Wireless World* that at an orbit of 36,000 kilometers (22,300 miles) the time for a satellite to circle the earth would exactly equal the 24-hour rotation of the earth. (That orbit bears Clarke's name today.) At that height, the satellites would be geostationary — always over the same equatorial point — and, if three were deployed 120 degrees apart, television and telephone signals could be easily connected worldwide.

4. My favorite historical footnote in all this relates to the guys hired by the Western Union Telegraph Expedition to lay out the telegraph line across Alaska and Siberia in the 1860's. The line never happened, because the trans-Atlantic line worked. George Kennan, told to twiddle his thumbs waiting for the Atlantic cable to fail, wrote *Tent Life in Siberia*, and later exposed inhumanities in Siberia's exile system. Naturalist William Healy Dall came to Alaska with George Kennicott, paid for by the telegraph expedition. Now, species of sheep and porpoise here bear Dall's name, and the large glacier and nearby copper mine in the Wrangell St. Elias region of Alaska were both named for Kennicott.

5. Lt Governor of Alaska, 2010-2014; Commissioner and Chair, U.S. Arctic Research Commission 2001-2010 (chair 2006-2010); founder and/or officer of several technology firms including Tundra Telephone, Nextel Alaska, Digimarc, Immersive Media, Venture Ad Astra, Zulu Time; Co-chair, State Committee on Research, which founded the Alaska Innovators Hall of Fame. Contact meadwell@alaska.net

THE AUTHOR

After living and working in rural Alaska during the 1970s, Alex Hills became a university professor. He is now Distinguished Service Professor at Carnegie Mellon University and Affiliate Distinguished Professor at the University of Alaska. He has also held distinguished visiting professor positions in Singapore, New Zealand, and Chile.

Dr. Hills is well known in the fields of wireless, telecommunication, and networking technology, having lectured widely and published many papers and technical reports. He holds 18 patents, issued and pending, and his easy-to-understand articles in *Scientific American* and *IEEE Spectrum* have been enjoyed by readers worldwide. He led the team that built Carnegie Mellon's "Wireless Andrew" system, the world's first large Wi-Fi network. With this work, described in his book, *Wi-Fi and the Bad Boys of Radio*, he helped to create the vision of what Wi-Fi would later become.

Professor Hills has also lived and worked in many foreign countries. For example, he has mentored Carnegie Mellon students working in Chile, Ghana, Palau, the Philippines, Cook Islands,

Rwanda, and Peru, showing them how to apply the technology skills they've learned to meet the needs of people living in developing nations. The experiences of these students are detailed in the book, *Geeks on a Mission*, written by Dr. Hills and the students themselves.

He continues to work on projects in Alaska and lives there with his wife Meg, now a nurse practitioner. The couple has two adult daughters, Drs. Rebecca and Karen Hills.

Printed in the USA
CPSIA information can be obtained
at www.ICGtesting.com
LVHW071735291124
797893LV00016B/504